Praise for *Elysian Hills*

———

Elysian Hills is a love story about a mother and her stepson during the last days of her life. It is, however, more than a love story. It is a journal about what we can learn when living in the presence of dying. This quote stands out for me, "I can ponder how I might want to die all I want, but the only use in this is the way these thoughts clear the fog of my not entirely conscious approach to living now." Reading this book brings one present to the beauty of living as well as dying.

—Linda Alepin,
Transformational Leadership Consultant

———

Grief is brutal; it can come fast and hard, or can arrive slowly and periodically. Paul guides us through the numerous emotions coupled with grief, capturing the complexity of relations, situations, experiences, and positionality. He nudges us toward reflection on our grief process, in an approachable and intentional way, supporting us however we are, wherever we are, while demonstrating ways to get where we want to be.

—Dr. Jessica Heiges,
Senior Sustainability Consultant at Quantis

———

This book by my son Paul about the dying experience of my wife Mary Lou of forty-six years is a treasure for me. Thank you, Paul, for bringing this story to life and for our love for one another as dad, son, and most of all true friends and soulmates.

—William H. Schmidt,
Husband, Father, Grandfather

————

Facing many losses of dear friends and family members during Covid-19, I became increasingly intrigued by the stark contrast between life and death, questioning if new life could stem from loss. That led me to Paul. The vulnerability and care he brings in this frank conversation about living with death and dying make this warm and engaging book the kind of read that will stick with you for a long time.

—Xiaoan Li, PhD,
Senior Program Officer at the Fetzer Institute

———

Paul Schmidt has gifted us with intimate, beautiful storytelling of his own experiences of offering loving presence to a family member who chose conscious dying. With elegance and care woven into his insights and words, he invites us into a unique sacred space. He manages to hold and honor the journeys of the various members of the family involved in the story. He shines a light into a potentially difficult situation, revealing how attention to deathing and conscious dying can inspire conscious living. Deathing needs as much attention in our world as birthing, and this book is a precious and powerful offering to an important topic.

—Barbara Nussbaum,
Author and award winning changemaker

ELYSIAN HILLS

Embracing Life
Through
Conscious Dying

PAUL WILLIAM SCHMIDT

ILLUMIFY
MEDIA.COM

Elysian Hills

The views and opinions expressed in this book are those of the
author and do not necessarily reflect the official policy or position of
Illumify Media Global.

Published by
Illumify Media Global
www.IllumifyMedia.com
"Let's bring your book to life!"

Paperback ISBN: 978-1-959099-40-6

Typeset by Art Innovations (http://artinnovations.in/)
Cover design by Debbie Lewis

Printed in the United States of America

Disclaimer

All information here is provided in good faith, however we make no representation or warranty of any kind, express or implied, regarding the accuracy, adequacy, validity, reliability, availability, or completeness of any information provided.

The authors, editors, publisher, and principals, as well as any named or guest contributors, disclaim any liability or responsibility to any person or organization for any loss, damage, expense, fine, injury, or penalty that may arise or result from the use of any information, ideas, opinions and/or errors in this book. Any use of, or reliance on, information reflected in this book and related resources is solely the responsibility of the reader.

If you or someone you know is experiencing suicidal thoughts or a crisis, please reach out immediately to the Suicide Prevention Lifeline at 800-273-8255 or text HOME to the Crisis Text Line at 741741, or dial 988. These services are free and confidential.

Death without life is impossible
Life without death is meaningless

Contents

Preface xiv

Acknowledgments xvi

Introduction 1

Finding Life at Elysian Hills 4

Mary Lou and Me 9

Saying Goodbye 14

VSED (Voluntarily Stopping Eating and Drinking) 22

Pondering Dying 29

The Choice 32

Independence and Agency 37

Suicide, Homicide, and Just Plain Old Death 42

Gatekeeping, Sanctity, and Dignity 47

Our Daily Bread 51

Angels Among Us 54

Surrender and Grace 59

Self, Family, Community, Society, and the
    Oneness of It All. 63
Stories, Legacy, and Transformation. 66
Giving and Receiving. 70
New Life Flashing Before Old Eyes 74
Continuum 78
Holy Union 84
It Sounds Easy, Dying 86
Service 94
Time for a Popsicle 97
Digging Deeper 102
The Will to Live. 106
Unfinished Stories 112
Last Conversations. 119
Ready?. . . Set?. 124
The Brutality of Truth. 128
Waiting. 133
Embracing the Unknown. 141
Doors and Windows 147
What Do I Have to Lose? 150
Natural Causes. 154
The Sound of Silence. 158
Marking the Moment 161
Pancakes 164
Dust to Dust 166
The Celebration. 169
In the End, It's Just Death 174

Gone in a Flash 176

Dead but Not Gone. 181

Denying Death and Change. 186

The Meaning of Life. 190

The Burden of Being Alive. 193

Love. 197

Communication with the Dead 200

My New Dad. 206

Epilogue. 210

Afterword 216

About the Author 219

Preface

———

About twenty-five years ago I had a year that included an experience with death once per month for twelve months in a row. Like some cosmic clock, from my grandfather to my housemate's father, wife's beloved calico cat, best friend's dog, three children, two babies, a coworker, and others.

Each passing was unique, from natural aging to euthanasia, accidents, suicide, chromosomal failure, heart attack, and miscarriage. My varied relationships and roles with each offered a profound mosaic of perspectives on loss and love. I've come to consider this my 101 level learning in the school of life's study of living with death.

The years of 2021 and 2022 were another such period riddled with fourteen or more deaths, framing my life with a continual presence of profound loss. This time, my learning edges emerged in deeper currents through nearly traumatic exposure to the process and experience of dying as well as losing and beginning to rediscover myself through layers and layers of grief.

I've learned much from these many varied encounters with death and continue to find new insights and self-affirmation every time I choose to look again and revisit one of these events.

This book follows one remarkable story, what happened, and how it changed me. There are no conclusions or formulas here, just a sharing of something unspeakable and without any need for resolution in my experience of coming to see death as one source of personal transformation which I could never be blessed to receive any other way.

I have a profound hope that reading this serves to connect you with your own experience in ways that are healing. I also hold this offering as the start to a conversation and would love to hear from you if you are at all compelled to reach out.

Perhaps together, we can celebrate how our world is more compassionate, peaceful, healthy, and alive when we choose to share more openly about life's lessons and gifts in death.

Acknowledgments

———

This book would not have been possible without the steadfast friendship and editorial coaching from Anne Messervy and her partner Manu. The care and encouragement they provided as I found the courage to write and share this story is evidence for me that the world is filled with goodness and that our collective drive to make a positive difference is unstoppable.

Also, I have deep appreciation for my many friends and colleagues who shared the journey by reading early drafts and providing invaluable feedback and reflections: Linda Alepin, Camilla Cartwright, Adrianne Chapman, Tim Clark, Sue Elliott, Dave Gibson, Jessica Heiges, Bruce Hennessey, Julia Kathleen, Xiaoan Li, Barbara Nussbaum, and my loving wife Kathy Morgan.

Lastly, it is with heartfelt gratitude and joy that I thank my dad Bill Schmidt for his support on so many levels in making this book honest, accurate, and financially possible.

Introduction

—

When losing a loved one, I've come to see each experience as a unique and precious opportunity to embrace life. The longer I live, the more frequently these chances to grow arise. This book is an exploration of some of what I've observed and learned through witnessing and supporting people and their loved ones as they die.

In fact, writing it was one way, selfishly, for me to attempt to discover myself anew following two years of ceaseless loss and grief. I hope in reading you too will become more comfortable with the wonder and joy (yes, joy) that can accompany the truth of death and dying.

This book follows the story of my stepmother Mary Lou's intentional ending of her life. She wasn't sick. There was no terminal condition. Death wasn't "knocking on her door." She had simply come to decide she was ready to let her physical body go and didn't want to wait any longer.

Simple but not easy, she chose, with great compassion for her husband (my dad) and those around her, to voluntarily stop eating and drinking as her path. All told, it took forty-four days for the process to unfold, and my dad and I, as willing participants, did our best to make the last days and weeks together with her as compassionate and honorable as possible.

My experiences navigating this auspicious time are still so vivid as all poignant life events are. Even after over a year and a half now I recall what happened as if it were last week.

As you read this, many of the indelible lessons Mary Lou's life has left me with will emerge. I sincerely hope you will find new clarity and a sense of deeper satisfaction in how you are choosing to live.

This experience revealed for me how death can be a source—perhaps the only direct one—to living with more love and compassion now. And in honoring any sense of duty to myself and my family, community, society, or the planet, the only place to start each new day is in cultivating loving relationships.

If you have experienced the death of a loved one or find yourself anticipating such an ending, I am sincerely sorry for your loss. I could never know what you're facing as you approach each death you may be confronted with, but I am clear that sharing about our journeys with regard and reverence is one way to keep track of joy and purpose along the way.

With respect, I've brought care in leaving many questions open and alive for you to consider for yourself in the privacy of your own reflections. I'd like to think this helps to nurture the possibility of bringing your best self to each unique conversation or experience of dying that lies ahead for you.

I recognize how deeply this topic touches each of us and am honored that along with all you are going through, you are choosing courage to take time and be thoughtful in facing it. In this way, this book will become your companion as you cultivate peace and healing for yourself and those closest.

It is my intention that reading this will inspire and equip you to mine for gifts from any death you have or will experience that become endless sources of joy and connection with yourself and others. I have a feeling that as you discover these gems and carry them with you, the ways they become polished and shine throughout the rest of your life will make the world a better place.

To join my mailing list and receive notice of events related to this book and new releases, please send me an email at paulschmidtauthor@gmail.com or visit the website for this book at elysianhillsbook.com

Finding Life at Elysian Hills

———

Elysian Hills is the name of a 140-acre farm in southern Vermont, a diverse haven of woods and fields nestled in the green mountain state's lush rolling hills, the land Mary Lou, my stepmother, called home and a literal extension of her physical being. She sensed a spiritual energy of connection immediately as the farmhouse came into view when approaching the property with her realtor in the late 1950s.

Mary Lou had been raised under the heavy hand of a misogynistic father in rural Pennsylvania. Born in 1927, seven or eight years after the youngest of her three siblings, she navigated her upbringing at a sprawling estate farm named Lockerby largely on her own. This context spurred her independent spirit, and she found her way to being the head of her own life and family with little to tie her to her heritage there.

As a strong young woman in her thirties, she ventured north to Vermont and quickly came to find and fall in love with the property that is now Elysian Hills. Initially, she and her first husband lived in the farmhouse, which was already more than 160 years old having been erected in 1791, as tenants renting from the estate of Ruth Knapp.

Ruth was the last heir in a family that had accumulated the various properties making up the farm 135 years earlier. Through three or more generations, the Knapp family had worked the land as one of many "hill farms" common in the area. The remnants of stone fences and maple sap collection tanks can still be found in the woods as evidence of their trade in one of the state's prized agricultural products, maple syrup. Census records also reveal their production of various crops including tobacco and likely corn and hay for livestock feed.

In an act of defiance to her father, Mary Lou purchased the Knapp Farm at the start of the 1960s and settled in, building a barn, tack shop, and riding arena and clearing pastures for a Morgan horse operation. Horses were mostly Mary Lou's thing, and as the first official American breed, Morgans had originated in Vermont as stunningly beautiful, well mannered, smart animals well suited to everything from farm work to pleasure riding and competition. Mary Lou grew the operation to provide breeding, training, and sales of horses and all related tack and supplies. Their Morgans won English, Western, Pleasure, and Trail Riding shows and became known in the region for their quality. Notably, a couple of years after starting the horse farm, state legislation was passed naming the Morgan horse Vermont's state animal.

All this while also raising three children. At first Mary Lou named the farm "Tamarlei," a portmanteau of her children's names. During the early seventies, when they had reached adulthood and she and her first husband divorced, Mary Lou sought a new name for the farm to fit her new life. Her sense of destiny in having been drawn to this place and the depth of connection she had sown in shouldering its stewardship offered her a sense of eternal beauty that transcended any idea of ownership. She felt the need to honor this truth as she had grown to see herself as having been brought into the world specifically to tenderly care for this place throughout and beyond her own life. And so she felt the term *elysian fields*, the Greek name for the home of the blessed after death, expressed the feeling that she had found paradise. With a typical Mary Lou twist of wit and wry factuality, she named the farm Elysian Hills, because "it was more hills than fields," she said.

By the mid-seventies she met Dad, another act of grace. A hard-working minister turned public servant who grew up in Buffalo New York, my dad is a gentle soul, always seeking new perspectives and driven to do good for others. As an able-bodied man, a life of working the land suited him in balance to his work founding and running the first regional planning commission in Vermont, and later, the Vermont Land Trust, an iconic institution standing for land-based planning and conservation.

Meeting and falling in love with my dad affirmed for Mary Lou her calling to steward the farm for life and beyond, now with a loving and capable partner who shared her value for putting the land first. As a testament to this strong bond, Mary Lou came to speak of everything that happened after marrying Dad as her "second life" and the best part of the whole thing hands down. Together they grew many crops at scale, from asparagus and other vegetables to a unique strain of rhubarb of which much was sold to a neighboring orchard and crafted into surprisingly tasty rhubarb wine. They brought a remarkable rutabaga-turnip hybrid, mild and delightfully sweet in taste, back from near extinction and established it as a certified heirloom botanical, harvesting its seed and selling it in all fifty states. The Gilfeather Turnip eventually became Vermont's state vegetable.

In over forty years of active farming and woodland management, Elysian Hills was recognized as an award-winning Vermont tree farm, offering a shining example of holistic woodland management with commercial Christmas trees, maple sugarbushes, red and white pine stands, hiking and skiing trails, a labyrinth, clearcutting for insect and wildlife habitat, stone tree creations, and a family circular stone cemetery.

While ownership of the land was deeded along with perpetual conservation restrictions to another local farmer in 2014, it retained the name Elysian Hills, and by agreement Mary Lou and Dad could live out their lives there and be buried in the cemetery they prepared on the property.

So, the roots of place-centered meaning for Mary Lou's life and death had been growing for more than sixty of her ninety-four years by the time she passed. A big cornerstone of her life journey was already complete in knowing exactly how and where she wanted her body to be laid to rest. Through this declaration that she had already found her version of heaven on earth, the energy of anticipation for leaving her body as she went on to discover whatever came next for her soul journey was full of wonder and invitation. She lived with peace with this understanding that "down here" on the physical plane, Elysian Hills would live on, and "up there," wherever that is, so would she.

For my part, in returning to visit Elysian Hills over more than forty-five years now, I've spent countless hours working side by side with Dad in support of the farm's care and purpose. The beauty of its spirit has become a cherished backdrop for my life and relationship with my father. I'm grateful for all that has unfolded through my dance with the eternal life force of Elysian Hills and touched my life as Mary Lou's stepson.

Mary Lou and Me

———

"Be sincere, even if you don't really mean it."
Chuck Pyle

As you read this, you'll come to know and understand my deep love and appreciation for Mary Lou. For me to be able to feel and express that now is a genuine joy. To be honest though, we didn't always have that kind of relationship while she was alive.

I was ten years old when we met, and it's hard to express the nature of our initial relationship because we didn't really want to have one to begin with, neither of us. She didn't like being around kids, and I wasn't supposed to like her anyway, according to my mom. Dad's choices had thrown us together, like it or not, and this wasn't a circumstance that motivated either of us to run and hug each other with joy.

In truth, I was mostly scared of her. Her frank and direct style felt threatening to me. To "have to" be around a person who wielded such strength of opinion insistent on things going her way was something to endure and survive.

To say we didn't care about each other is inaccurate, for we also didn't not care and, as incomplete as that sounds, that was really it for at least the first twenty-five years or so. For me, when I visited Elysian Hills, it was about spending time with Bill (what I called my father then. This shifted to Dad sometime when I was in college) and I think for her, having me around was only acceptable out of a similar obligation. As long as we were civil with each other everything was tolerable, and we always were.

Given the chance to share in this way here, I can now see how what did take root for us only revealed its sweetness as it grew more at the speed of a glacier forming than spurred by mutual attraction and the fire of shared passion. Perhaps my own shortcomings didn't give her credit enough, but to me she extended interest and shared in celebrating my accomplishments mostly because it was important to Dad. Likewise, I brought myself to pay attention to her and open to listening and learning about who she was more because she and Dad came as a package, yoked in marriage and common purpose by their own brand of dedication and commitment to walking through life together.

Any shame I may have felt along the way for not doing more than show up when I had to and be quietly respectful in my interactions with her was my own private experience. I don't know how it really was for her, for we never discussed it directly, but the best way I can hold it now is that we each found, over our long history of brief interactions and hearing about each other through Dad, that we could bring our hearts to the table and it would be reciprocated. We allowed any propensity to avoid or not trust the other one to be there without much strife, probably each knowing that these traits of tentative aloofness were artifacts of habit stemming more from our separate pasts than having anything to do with our lives together.

It wasn't till well into my forties that our relationship became more direct and intentional. She started occasionally seeking my advice with issues she was grappling with. Whether it was which button to press on the computer or a more personal quandary with Dad or one of her children, I always did my best to be both thoughtful and diplomatic with my reflections and suggestions.

In the few years before she passed, she carefully and confidentially sought my counsel with more intricate concerns emerging around Dad: how best to navigate her fear of his waning driving competency was one question that particularly challenged her. Another was his joy in using his chainsaw alone in the woods and the obvious risks involved. I found myself in an ultimately humorous position often when she would lead a conversation with "Don't tell your dad, but. . . " and then later that same day, when out working in the woods, Dad would say, "Don't tell Mary Lou that I'm using the chainsaw." Maintaining my own integrity while respecting each of their confidences was an interesting challenge.

As obstinate and broken as we both were, we eventually came to know each other as good people who shared a drive for honest positive living, wanting only the best for others. No family members were harmed along the way with Mary Lou and me and while that may seem pathetic to settle for, it honestly occurs as a profound accomplishment.

In writing this story, it's almost surprising that I've been able to realize and acknowledge the depth of love expressed in these pages. But the uplifting sense of relief I have in doing so is evidence enough for me that it was always there. Even though we might well have chosen to be more active or explicit in sharing it directly while she was alive, it's completely okay that we mostly didn't.

The more I was able to learn about her past and how experience shaped her, the more my admiration and awe grew. I had always believed my dad when he spoke of her amazing and worthy qualities and could now see them for myself. As easy as it is for a child to judge parental figures for things they don't yet have the capacity to understand, it is affirming when two people age together well and eventually embrace a more peer level of mutual acceptance as adults.

I definitely don't miss Mary Lou in her death like Dad does. More profound to me is the lasting impact of who she was for me that has come into perspective mostly since she passed. From my numerous experiences with dying loved ones so far, being able to celebrate someone in their death no matter what colors may have painted our living relationship is now more like a muscle worth exercising for me, an opportunity to get over myself and be bigger than our collective humanness that I know well enough to tend to before people pass.

Saying Goodbye

———

"It's the emptiest and yet the fullest of
all human messages: 'Good-bye.'"
Kurt Vonnegut

When someone close to me is dying, I don't always get the chance to say goodbye directly. I've learned that having that opportunity and acting on it doesn't fill the void that appears when confronting the loss part of change. But when I have risked sharing openly from my heart when present to the fact that this may very well be the last chance I have, I've always been surprised at the sense of freedom and lightness that arrives. It's as if by affirming the connection in a relationship, however it is right then and however the words come out in that moment, the tension of holding things unsaid in a relationship dissolves, opening the space where the expanse of interconnectedness lives as shared experience and words really don't matter much.

I now know that any conversation I'm having now is the only one that really matters, whether it ends up being the last or not, and it's okay to share from my heart any time. And. . . knowing that it is likely the last one ahead of time, while sometimes difficult, is an uncommon and precious opportunity.

> *Dear Mary Lou,*
>
> *I hope you get this message and are able to receive it privately as it is intended to be from my heart to yours.*
>
> *When I got the call from [your son] and learned of your decision, I was briefly surprised and very quickly filled with a huge sense of admiration and awe and gratitude for you. I completely 'get it' regarding the various components that went into your decision and can see how much of a relief it must be to have found a path that works for you. The bold courage and unabashed love for yourself and everyone close to you in taking this step is truly inspired.*
>
> *Thank you.*
>
> *And bless you. I am no stranger to death and dying, especially this year, and am happy to be able to be of service (without over-*

whelming anyone with my agendas, of course!) in any way I can. I appreciate your message regarding requesting my presence in support of Dad through this remarkable transition. I am making plans to be out there by next weekend. I don't know if I'll get to see you before your physical life comes to a gentle close or not, so I'll make this my last communication to you with an unattached hope to maybe give you one last hug.

Also, please know that I will be completely responsible for getting the Peony to Bonnie if that hasn't happened before I arrive. . . :)

I'm happy to attempt a phone call any time if you would like, but given the challenges with volume and shared company, I thought a written message would be sufficient. Up to you though on that. Please call any time if you're so moved.

What else?? So much, and so little need to say anything really. For me, that is a sign that we have a healthy and pure relationship and for that I am so grateful. I know you know I love you. I know you know that I am dedicated to and capable of supporting Dad in whatever unfolds for him in the coming days/weeks/months and hopefully years. I'll do my best to help him sort out what to keep close and what to let go of and let change as he navigates a very different life, at least on a day-to-day level.

I think I'll leave this here for now and thank you. Thank you for being a strong Stepmom and even stand-in mom for me over the years. Thank you for being so dedicated to the power of place and conscious stewardship of Elysian Hills. Thank you for being a beautiful life partner for Dad both in this life and others past and probably yet to come. I am filled by who you have been for me in ways that will never die and know that pieces of you will continue to live through in the world as I find new ways to spread integrity, joy, and a gracious example of what's truly right in the world. Thank you.

I wish you the very best in these magical last few days or weeks. It is a special time to be so alive and I hope that you and Dad can indulge in being together as you tend to the basic human needs along with the profoundly simple moments of just sitting together.

If you're around past Saturday, the 18th, I'll see you then! If not, good for you!

*And I'll look forward to seeing you in spirit
and beyond.*

*Congratulations on a life so well lived
and Godspeed (strangely appropriate sentiment) as you find the doorway to beyond.*
With love,
Paul

————

It was two days before I sent that email when my stepmother shared with my dad over breakfast that she had
decided to stop eating and drinking as a pathway to completing her physical life. I learned of the news a few hours
later from my stepbrother, who had rarely if ever phoned
me before then. At the time, I was standing in the middle
of the desert wilderness of the San Rafael Swell in central
Utah, having just arrived to enjoy a week of fall camping
with seven family members and friends and two dogs.

When I saw the name pop up on my iPhone, I took a
breath before carefully swiping to answer. In his practical
and matter-of-fact way, he informed me of his mom's decision and that he was calling to relay her request that I do
my best to find "a few days" to travel to Vermont and look
after my dad during the transition.

Two years earlier, my stepbrother and I had connected one on one, for the first time I think, in our parents'

forty-six years of marriage. He was shuttling me to an early flight from Bradley International Airport to return home to Wyoming after helping out for a month during my dad's recovery from double knee replacement surgery. Because of Mary Lou's advanced age compared to Dad (she was eight years older), and her accelerated physical deterioration primarily related to her multiple sclerosis, we knew then that a time would likely come soon when Mary Lou would leave Dad. That day we made a brotherly pact to be there to "catch" him as he grappled with the loss.

So, the call wasn't too much of a surprise, but the circumstances briefly caught me off guard. Having no direct prior experience or even knowledge of such an act of determination and courage as inviting one's death in this way, the questions began to flood my mind and soul. In a flash of insight, I quickly realized who we were talking about and replied, with a muddled laugh, "Of course! This is exactly how Mary Lou would have it."

He chuckled in wholehearted agreement, for if his mom could be described with just one outstanding quality it was that she was always in control and happiest when also in charge, direct in her dealings with anyone, and unabashedly in the driver's seat of her life albeit with tact for those around her.

It was a quality that she wore well for those who didn't get triggered by it. I certainly did in the past, decades ago when we were both younger. But with the benefit of maturity and the mandate that being family provides, a mutual reverence had grown between us that tempered our separate brands of stubbornness enough to have let us move beyond any fear of conflict and just be ourselves together.

She had been carefully weighing myriad factors regarding her deteriorating quality of life and increasing burden on Dad and those around her. I would come to learn more later about the real-world options available to someone in her position, ready to die on a conscious soul level before her biological form was. But she had come to this path as the only course she could take to be able to go with integrity, honesty, and grace. For her, it was as much a gift to her loved ones as it was a solution to her conundrum, an ultimate realization of her living wishes.

We all knew that this was a highly conscious and calculated decision and that she would not waver.

A year earlier, I had co-facilitated a three-day retreat exploring the topic of death and renewal with forty deeply conscious and beautiful people. At the time, my own mother was unwell, and I was vaguely aware of the foreshadowing confirmed as the next two years of immersion in the experience of witnessing one death after another took shape. Beginning with having been at my mother's side as she passed gently on a full moon just nine bewildering months before Mary Lou's decision, the rest of 2021 and 2022 revealed the occasion to learn about, support to varying degrees, and grieve fourteen other significant deaths, including Mary Lou's.

So, following the call to come to Mary Lou and Dad's aid, I quickly slipped into a practiced, familiar, and even welcome role of compassionate supporter. Girding my emotions, opening my heart, and tuning my awareness, I set about making plans to cut the desert time short and get my butt back east with a looming sense that the wrenching and beautiful events of my past year had been a training of sorts for supporting Dad and Mary Lou.

Upon arriving at Elysian Hills, any dread or anticipation I had melted thankfully when I entered their radiant bubble of light and joy. There were my dad and his beloved wife, doing their thing, almost as always but apparently energized by the ethereal quality of finality shining new light on all the formerly mundane routines in their day.

Mary Lou's biggest concern in dying was how it would affect Dad. She wanted her passing to be a gift of freedom for him and could step around any selfish desire to stay here with him in their love and life together only for knowing that he could find the strength to flourish beyond the trauma of being left behind.

She knew I shared this concern and a commitment to supporting Dad however I could. We had talked about it over the years and we both knew that my role would be of paramount importance in this regard during her dying and beyond.

It was from here that I joined Mary Lou and Dad's remarkable journey.

VSED (Voluntarily Stopping Eating and Drinking)

Yes, there's an acronym for the act of stopping eating and drinking. Who knew?

I found it fairly easy to get through the initial sensations of hunger whenever I've intentionally fasted. For a stretch while in college I engaged in three-day fasts twice a month and came to look forward to the experience. Resisting my body's urge to eat was a small act of deferral for the gratification of so many benefits. I would experience clarity of thought, seemingly endless energy, and an ability to focus that freed my mind from the typical swirls of self-doubt and worry I habitually indulged in.

On a practical level as a time and money-starved student it was easy to temporarily enjoy the savings in not having to purchase, prepare, and eat food. I came to view the necessity of consumption as a thick filter dimming my access to conscious connection with the universe as

I navigated simple three-day fasts with only water in the middle, bookended by juice on the first and last days. Once, I extended the experience with an open-ended timeline and found the fire in my soul burned bright and with increasing clarity for about a week before my body began to weaken and my mind confused.

Given my firsthand experiences of fasting, Mary Lou's decision to stop eating was easier to relate to for me than for Dad. I understood how she could continue to join us in the dining room at mealtimes to feed on the opportunity for connection and sharing, even if the ritual of breaking bread together had been broken. In the first weeks, she continued the regular schedule of shared dining with friends and family, the regular Sunday morning breakfasts at the Flamingo Diner and even a "last supper" of sorts with family at their usual table at the New England House in West Brattleboro.

Witnessing Mary Lou's continued presence at shared meals was an affirmation of the fortitude of her clarity. She was at peace with her decision and welcoming of the mystery of the process about to unfold. While this may have seemed strange to others, I think we all felt a measure of comfort in how dining without eating was a way for her to put her choice into action. Seeing her embrace the treasured time shared over meals was a way to affirm for ourselves that this was really happening, as the joy of being together was inescapable.

Not drinking, however? This was another story.

Unlike fasting, I have never willingly sought out the experience of dehydration. While I probably never drink enough water each day, the handful of times I've ventured too far into the abyss of dehydration have been fraught with confusion, anxiety, and an unspeakable, base, and visceral drive to find water.

I recall the second day of an ascent of Washington's Column (a "big wall" in Yosemite) when my rock-climbing partner and I were moving as quickly as we could safely in a race against weather and then daylight. We chose not to take the time to dig through our haul bag of gear for water, and as the hours of exertion passed, I became delirious with thirst. Pushing ourselves with youthful determination at least ten hours after our last sip, we arrived at a drop-off near the end of the technical part of the descent. It was almost too dark to see if it was too far to jump or not. We chose to toss the haul bag, an army duffel containing eighty pounds or more of gear, because a) we knew we couldn't get ourselves down carrying the "pig" (technical term), b) we had to move quickly, and c) with any luck we might hear when it landed and better understand what to do next. The duffel disappeared into the shadows of evening and basically exploded on impact. Once we got down to collect and repack the contents, each of us separately came across a full one-liter water bottle and remarkably, without any thought of finding the other to share, or any reasoning or communication at all, we each drank our entire bottle in one go. The water did wonders for my energy, but I was still thirsty. I remember noticing the next morning, some eight or so hours later, after making it to camp, having a spaghetti (waterlogged noodles) dinner, and much more water, that my body hadn't yet received enough excess to have to urinate. In this case, and others, different from the navigable dance with will and conscious choice that going without food presented, nothing could have stopped me from drinking as soon as I possibly could.

Ignorant of the nuances involved with intentional dehydration and taking what I had heard of her decision at face value, I had confirmed that a body without water can only be expected to survive a matter of days or perhaps a week at most. Given Mary Lou's existing physical frailty, having lost most of her mobility in her forty-plus years living with MS, I didn't expect her to break any records and had prepared myself for the prospect of her departing before my arrival. When I did first see her, more than a week since her declaration, I was both relieved and immediately taken aback by her verve and vigor. She was beaming, alert, smiling, overflowing with conversation, and eager to see me.

And she had a popsicle in a dish by her chair. . .

I didn't say anything at first out of respect and to give myself time to sort out my own ideas around this fact. I had come girded for the yeoman's task of watching someone suffer their last days and hours as gracefully as possible, and while it was a relief that that part wasn't at hand yet, I was conflicted on how to have integrity in supporting her and be compassionate at the same time.

Gently approaching the subject with my dad, I got a glimpse of his own flirtations with denial of the finality of Mary Lou's spoken desire to die and none too soon. "Popsicles aren't food," he said, "and she's not drinking anything except a little water at night to keep her mouth moist."

I had never expected this to be a straightforward process, but I went to bed that first night clear that my role and presence was going to test my capacity for tact and discretion beyond perhaps anything I had ever experienced before. My more natural feminine instincts prohibited me from settling for too much literality in the execution of this project. But my masculine drive couldn't let go of skilled tunnel vision in applying discipline and focus on the goal as a critical piece of ultimate honor and success.

After all, considering the possibilities of what might happen should she abandon the process at any point was untenable, mostly for the crushing confrontation with failure this would surely invite on an emotional level, and how quickly the desire to die would return, likely with even more determination and very possibly less rationality.

I couldn't think about that. Mary Lou was determined and seemed to understand what was at stake, but I wasn't sure about Dad. While he was wholeheartedly in support of her wishes it was also clear that, perhaps from not wanting their life together to end yet or perhaps from natural denial in such situations, he would have welcomed any reversal of course on her part. I understood this, as it had been her decision not his, and to support her fully, he would need to "get on board" for himself. I knew this would take time and be helped by keeping the reality of what we were facing clear and present through talking about the blunt truth of his wife dying soon and asking questions that helped him prepare.

While it may seem unfair for Mary Lou to have sprung this decision on Dad the day she started, the truth was quite the opposite. She was very careful and compassionate in not discussing how serious she was growing about dying with intention before she took action. This was clear as she went out of her way with me and many others to confirm that this was *her* decision, not Dad's. She wanted to leave no room for anyone to make up the idea that Dad wanted this, lobbied for it, or had anything to do with "getting rid of her."

I could only begin to appreciate how this very odd yet sensible act of love was shocking for Dad. It would take a bit for him to sort out his feelings and discover the possibility of gratitude for her decision. This would all have to happen mostly in private for him as the call to support her wholeheartedly preempted integrating what it meant for him.

If he felt betrayed at all, I would have understood, but he didn't show any of that. The truth was that they had always made major decisions together for over forty years now, and not only was this one of the few made separately, but it would also leave him in the unfamiliar place of making all future life decisions on his own going forward.

Fortunately, their relationship already included the capacity to talk about aging, death, and dying.

Pondering Dying

———

*"To the well-organized mind, death is but
the next great adventure."*
J.K. Rowling

A healthy level of conversation around aging and dying has been very much out in the open and a common topic in our family. This was good in that so many of the logistical parts were largely already planned. Beyond that, I knew that being aware of their more "spiritual" (my word), "*not* religious" (Mary Lou's) beliefs and style of understanding how a soul lives in relationship to the body would help the three of us navigate this part of the journey together with a welcome sense of intimate alignment at least on a thought level.

"I'm not afraid of dying." My dad has said this frequently in recent years. Whether affirming it into being or for some other reason, he was compelled to share this thought.

From what I could tell, fear wasn't remotely part of Mary Lou's concern. I remember her breaking a moment of silence at the dinner table following a family reunion-style event eight years earlier with a smile and the words "Okay. Can I go now?" She was joking at the time, but in being so free to do so the undercurrent of her level of acceptance and even growing eagerness was clear. So, we knew she had been ready and waiting for a while. Now she was taking action, and this was new territory for all of us.

My connections with Mary Lou and Dad regarding personal matters and emotional sharing each had a separate flavor to it. But observing them together I came to trust that while they talked about matters of spirit more in the context of practical implications, they were aligned and most comfortable leaving each other to their own on the deeper stuff.

I recognized a fear or concern I had though, that this tendency to dwell more in the head and leave matters of the heart mostly unspoken would create a tension for me against my own style of being more explicit in discussing the emotional and energetic aspects of the experience consciously as we went. In any case, my decades of work as a therapeutic body/energy worker had trained me in the art of providing support while keeping mostly in the background. This prepared me with a level of skill and comfort in letting all that be.

I quietly entered the sanctity of this space with Mary Lou and Dad with keen awareness that most of what was meaningful would not, could not, and didn't need to be discussed directly. The proxies of metaphor, sharp wit, and momentary eye contact beyond words where souls embrace in mutual understanding would be more than enough to serve my purpose and theirs.

I was in awe of the tender sweetness of two people who had grown entwined in acceptance, each giving full license to the other to have their own ideas without any obligation to share anything that wasn't meant to be aired out even between life partners. Secrets taken to the grave? Perhaps. But more than that, for nothing seemed secret, just a simple unspoken pact of respect and grace.

The Choice

—

"Today is the first day of the rest of my life."
John Denver

By stopping eating and drinking, Mary Lou had chosen to die, or I think more accurately, chosen to invite an inevitability to her dying very soon as her next act. For her, it was more of a plan or project that by design had a fairly certain outcome if the strategy was employed fully. To die was inevitable, and all she could do was speed up the process. Her death would come later.

So, I saw how I too could choose to die. It's easy to grant myself that power over my biological design to continue living until I don't, or power over any will of my family or community to deny my dying through medical intervention or other artificial means. But could I choose to live? I'd have to think more about that and wade through questions like: How might I have already stopped living?

Why am I here? What would/could I live for? And why does any of it matter?

I've come to see how Mary Lou paradoxically wanted to die but hadn't yet given up on living. Her decision to stop eating and drinking wasn't simply a choice to die at all. It was much more a choice to live now. . . and not for long.

Her chosen path was an act of beginning the rest of her life with freedom from any conflict or burden from an open-ended (seemingly endless?) wait. It was an unburdening of the need to plan and strive for anything long term that she might be part of. As the days grew to weeks and then to more than a month, her desire to die continued to plague her, for it was all still taking too long.

Always determined in doing everything for herself that she could and not accepting help until she decided she wanted it turned out to be a core trait and one of the last to go. Both a willful quality of being and nearly instinctual urge, it was the key to her ability to decide to die as well as an impediment to the process happening with more haste.

She would bristle if, with the best of chivalrous intentions, I tried to close the car door or open the door to the house for her. Accepting my helpful intentions was eclipsed by her adamance in not wanting to appear helpless or be dependent on others. Later on, when these tasks were too risky or difficult, my help was welcome, and she would politely thank me for my assistance. I could tell it was hard for her though. Given my propensity to help before being asked and her fierce independence of feminine power and fire, we'd had many opportunities to do this dance and over time, I had learned how not to step on her toes.

Two years earlier I'd lived with them for a month while my dad was recovering from double knee replacement surgery, picking up daily duties like preparing meals, making the bed, driving to doctor's appointments or social engagements, and the like. I did my best in being mindful to provide a familiar environment yet stay out of their way as much as possible, especially once the novelty of my visiting wore off after a few days.

I remember preparing the tray of before-dinner drinks, cheese, and crackers one evening. When I went to announce that it was time to join and share conversation before dinner, Mary Lou, just getting herself out of her chair and preparing to navigate the hallway with her walker to the kitchen, snapped, saying she was coming to get the tray together as that was her job, a clear message that my presence was becoming intrusive even for all the "help" I was offering. Not needing to take her ire personally (thank goodness) I responded with an apology, stating that it would be great if she prepared the tray, and thank you. In the time it took her to reach the kitchen, I was able to quickly pour all the drinks back into their containers and return the crackers and cheese to their boxes in the cupboard and fridge. As she arrived, I left for a walk outside, to give her (and me) the space we each needed to let the outburst pass as she went about preparing the tray herself.

It wasn't about the food. I knew she didn't like behaving or talking *at* me that way but that she didn't have a choice, given her level of stress at having their routines interrupted. Moreover, I could see she was probably wondering, with a measure of fear, if my dad's recovery would be sufficient to allow him to continue caring for her in the ways they had grown comfortable with.

This dynamic surfaced again somewhere around three or four days before she died as the administering of medications became a battleground of sorts. Not because she didn't want the medicine, but because she didn't want anyone to give it to her; she wanted to take it herself. The process of getting the contents from the syringe into her mouth and swallowed increasingly involved a struggle, as she would clamp her lips shut and grab at the syringe wanting to do it herself. But in her advanced delirium, she was mostly unable to get it done without missing her mouth entirely and dispensing the liquid everywhere but inside. Both Dad and I did our best to use as little force as possible and at one point I even started bringing a second empty syringe for her to grab at while I snuck the medicine in from the other side.

This example of insistence, self-determination, and remarkable strength led Jennifer, the hospice nurse, to exclaim to us as she left from a routine home health visit.

"Mary Lou's strength is amazing. I don't know for the life of me how that woman is still here. She fights like a copperhead in my backyard!" (Jennifer is from southern Georgia and you will need to go back and read that out loud in your best thick southern drawl to get the full effect of love and care with which it was delivered.)

Dad and I both knew we were there to assist, but that she would ultimately do the dying on purpose herself.

Independence and Agency

——

"I did it my way."
Frank Sinatra

Having things done for her wasn't Mary Lou's cup of tea. It wasn't that she had to do *everything* herself, just best when done on her terms. Most of us can relate to the value of agency as the action piece of affirming our worth in the world, and this is especially important for those of advanced age.

Living with deteriorating physical ability due to her MS and severe scoliosis, Mary Lou's challenge with maintaining independence was that her mobility had been increasingly compromised over the recent decades. Although she exercised her fullest capacity to embody physical action while acquiescent to her limitations, her strength of character and steadfast mental acuity disallowed any gratuitous help right up to the end. Mary Lou adapted processes that allowed her to do what needed to be done unaided and without complaint but was admirably able to concede control with gratitude when necessary. An OG exemplification of the empowered Woman, Mary Lou never martyred herself and had grown to favor strength of pride over any idea of being dependent.

When no longer able to navigate the uneven ground of her beloved hilly fields on foot to work the Christmas tree farm, she took to being the chief mower. She became a deft operator of the riding lawn tractor, continuing to contribute to the farm labor of love by keeping the miles of aisles among the rows of Christmas trees clear of tall grasses until she was eighty-seven.

Her use of a walker around town and eventually the house became more frequent, but still there were falls. With my dad as her faithful assistant, they worked out routines for things like getting her into the car. She would approach the front door and leave her walker at the threshold. Then, while she was working her way out and down the single granite block step with the assistance of the iron railing crafted by her blacksmith son, Dad would reposition the walker on the walkway where she would take over and shuffle, swinging her "dead leg" (as she called it) along as she made her way to the waiting car.

It was very important as the helper to not help too much as this angered her. She would shift herself from walker to open car door for support, position her feet carefully, and fall backward into the car seat in just the right way so as to avoid the need to reposition her butt. Then, giving the high sign, which was usually a nod, dad would "huck" her legs into the car with a single confident motion so as to minimize the pain of the movement. From there, she could lean forward and reach to close the door herself, put on her seatbelt and be ready to go.

So, while Dad was convalescing from knee surgery, I took over this role, and Mary Lou and I would venture out together in this way for her weekly massage and hair appointments and to the supermarket. On the Monday morning food shops, I quickly learned that the main reason we went early in the morning wasn't primarily to avail ourselves of freshly stocked shelves, but more to avoid unnecessary traffic in the store as she tore up and down the supermarket aisles on the motorized shopping cart.

Wasting no time, she dispatched the task of collecting items on her list, carefully itemized and cross referenced with an envelope of coupons clipped from the newspaper circular the previous day. In the driver's seat, she came alive with determination and a measure of joy in the freedom and efficiency she commanded behind the controls. Greeted by name by store staff preparing for the day of shoppers, I could tell they knew well enough to keep clear as she rarely used the slow speed, cornering, backing, and braking, always brushing stacks of product within inches but never running into anything.

We had all learned from experience that if you happened to find yourself in Mary Lou's way, that was your problem.

Over the prior recent years, her increasing reliance on Dad around the house just to get into bed or to the bathroom troubled her. My dad never complained and did his best to honor her need for privacy when bathing or dressing, only helping when absolutely necessary. But the risks of this lifestyle of mutual dependence only grew with increasing incidents of her collapsing to the floor and having to wait for his help, which had eventually become insufficient to lift her completely by himself.

They were a team. Between her sharpness of mind and his physical ability, they got it done. Mary Lou took her role seriously, keeping things on track mentally for the two of them. A few times she voiced her concern to me privately at how deciding to leave Dad to live alone would leave this "job description" unfulfilled as much as it would offer him a gift of freedom from the burden of care. She was asking me to take over as much as I could, watching out for Dad's increasing lapses in memory or attention. I assured her that I would, of course, do my best.

So while she was approaching death, this practiced process of co-designing solutions for tending to the most basic of daily needs accelerated in the final month. Her capacities were deteriorating rapidly enough to warrant new adaptations to routines as former strategies no longer worked. I was impressed with their acceptance of change, not before it was needed, but exactly when prudent.

At one point, with a simple phrase, she conceded to Dad that she would not be needing his help in using the wheelchair to go to the bathroom, that it was time to move from the chair to the hospital bed we had set up in the living room. Despite these being things they may have declared would never happen a couple of days earlier, they became so, without struggle or much discussion at all.

While I consider myself adept at change, witnessing this dance between a couple, performed with the perfection born of practice and simple grace, I wondered what my life could be like if I didn't belabor decisions so much, or if (heaven forbid!) I was able to better accept the help of others.

Suicide, Homicide, and Just Plain Old Death

———

"Our job is improving the quality of life,
not just delaying death."
Robin Williams

As the weeks progressed, I marveled at how an intimate encounter with the bizarre continuum of nuance regarding these words and their meaning unfolded.

With a lifetime of raw and poignant reference points for the varied disposition and experiential realities surrounding people as their lives end, I have found myself oddly comfortable with death. No wonder it is so common for many westerners to easily talk about the prospect of dying in the context of fear. While Buddhists actively practice dying on a daily basis in meditation, and so many other eastern and indigenous cultures celebrate the eminently temporary nature of the physical body, it seems vast numbers of humans less practiced with ritualizing the spiritual wonder of it all probably find the final sentences of the final chapter of life a bit overwhelming. . . that is, if we choose the gift of being present while it's happening.

There are differences between saying "I'm going to kill myself" and "I'm ready to die" and "Please help me die now." What I heard in Mary Lou's declaration, however, was an amazing blend of all these proclamations.

It's easy, on the surface, to see suicide as a self-directed act of ending one's life chosen by one who, for whatever reason, isn't up for the possibility of leaving with more responsibility and care for others. While I can have compassion and even maybe appreciation for choosing to act in this way, I can't get over a troubled sadness in the seeming selfishness of suicide. Sad since the choice feels like it short circuits the opportunity to share the process with others in a more loving way. I can get the feeling of being trapped in the totality of the idea that there is no other way, but what is lost in the bigger picture seems nothing short of tragic.

Writing this feels a bit messy, so clearly I probably have work I could do with myself on this topic, but for now what I know is that being ready to die, even wanting to in short order, is different from acting out of simply not being willing to live anymore.

When stripped of the context of whatever precipitating story results in the bold and frequently tragic decision to commit suicide, the clinical meaning of the word is "to harm oneself with the intent of causing death." My own first reaction to this is to balk at the word *harm* for this assumes that disrupting one's physical capacity to live is harmful. No doubt that makes sense from a reductionist perspective but what about "harm" to the soul that may endure for the act of preserving or continuing physical life?

All this subjectivity opens the door to a swirl of other terms which, as attempts to define and label a vast range of ultimately situational mosaics of experience, belief, and choice, inherently fall short of any conclusive clarity. Assisted suicide or death with dignity has four versions: active, passive, indirect, and physician assisted. Euthanasia is much less involved with the will of the dying. And even further subjectivity regarding the ways dying is affected arises on the continuum along which the separate goals of curative care, palliative care, and hospice care land.

Maybe it comes down to intent. That, and the granting of authority in the matter. Who gets to decide the how, what, and when of it all? When is it "right" for someone else to stop supporting someone's life? What is an unacceptable form of living? Is everyone concerned, doctors, nurses, family members aligned in how the person's intentions and desires are being interpreted?

The prospect of death as compared to the reality of dying touches each of us with such depth of feeling and consideration that any predetermined or planned path can be disrupted by a reconsideration of our innermost morals and ethics at any time, right up till the last breath.

While in the midst of this process with Mary Lou, it was clear that there was no solid or static ground for answering many of these questions. This is the nature of ethics in action. Fortunately, family members were clear and accepting of her choice and generally supportive, each in their own way.

As for the layer of details only revealed to those of us on close watch, the only place I could find any ability to be actively present and supportive was more of a dance with what was emerging. Continually checking in with an ever-changing landscape of context spanning all levels of factors, from the sometimes insane-feeling consideration of little things like how many ice chips to give her, to other choices like when another dose of morphine or lorazepam was in order, which had more profound existential-feeling implications.

For me, the missing piece of this whole conversation stems from the presumption that everyone involved is autonomous in agency in such matters. This then begs the question "Who has the authority to decide and take action?" I believe this is a false question. What if no "one" has authority? What if, in our natural interconnectedness where each participant's ideas are entwined with the others', such a decision is more of a fluid group process? How could it not be? This brings the task at hand more into a relationship space where the strengths and forces at play are woefully inexpressible objectively in words and qualities like presence, trust, love, fidelity, compassion, honor, and reverence paint the signposts on the journey.

In the moment, thankfully, I felt Dad and I a worthy and capable team at the core, as his penchant for head-level clarity and mine for heart-level integrity collectively seemed to at least stand a chance of supporting a satisfactory process. It wouldn't be easy or always joyful or without strife, but it could be ultimately whole and complete for all, I hoped. In any case, we accepted solidarity in being a team and offered each other strength in our courage to see things through, together, as best we could.

Gatekeeping, Sanctity, and Dignity

——

"We don't need to share the same opinions as others,
but we need to be respectful."
Taylor Swift

Then there were the opinions.

I also knew from other experiences that I had been called to serve as a gatekeeper of sorts, buoying the process on the shifting seas of emotions as their community of close friends, neighbors and family came and went. I knew those interactions would introduce a mix of varied capacity to address everything from the metaphysical and mystical to the blatantly practical for Mary Lou. And I endeavored to do my best to help each connection support the uniqueness of each relationship without disrupting Mary Lou's anticipated ups and downs along the way.

As humans, we are judging and assessing machines and everyone around Mary Lou had their own idea about what she was going through, along with each their unique confirmation and capacity to share it, sometimes couched in insightful or misplaced attempts at sensitivity, sometimes authoritatively intrusive, and occasionally delivered with enough self-awareness to invite worthy unanswerable questions. Mostly, when bumping into a neighbor on their daily walk or interfacing with Mary Lou's friends and family in the driveway, these candid conversations revealed more about their capacity to accept Mary Lou's display of clarity and courage in the reflection it offered for their own relationship with life and death.

If my role included "gatekeeping" (I don't know a better term), I took on a sense of obligation to be as tactful as possible in filtering the flood of good intentions for helping. Uncomfortable wielding such authority, I attempted to gently translate the energy for visitors so their presence could land with Mary Lou as love in a way that protected the sanctity of the space for her to reach the door on her own. This involved being as perceptive and as skillful as possible in reflecting for others' benefit. I did my best to offer opportunities to enter the temple, so to speak, with due respect and the chance to be transformed. This was about Mary Lou first, and I knew I had the capacity to cultivate a safe space for her to find the peace she was seeking and deserved.

I decided, as best I could, who could safely (for Mary Lou and/or my dad) be allowed in with their opinions and offerings, and who was best to keep outside or even send away.

At one point, I remembered that, just ten months earlier in my mom's case, we perceived that the presence of me and others seemed to be triggering her desire to stay here, hang on, and interact. While decidedly a judgment call in her advanced near-death state, we decided that letting go would be easier as a private experience for her with us supporters there more in spirit. I remembered sitting with her hours before she passed and letting her know that I was there but that I would no longer touch her or share in words. She was past any ability to respond coherently, but the gentle squeeze of my hand had to be reassurance enough for me that she understood and maybe, hopefully, was okay herself with this.

Dad and I discussed this, and one of the nurses even acknowledged how the occurrence of visitors with a hospice patient was a tradeoff, positive in providing access to completion and tending to relationships, but also with a cost of expending waning energy beyond what was comfortable and of keeping one's mind churning with activity not conducive to finding a peaceful departure.

So, at breakfast one morning I thought I heard my dad say, "No more visitors," out of having clearly crossed the line of what was helpful the day before. Certainly, it was time to stop people who were coming over more for their own benefit than Mary Lou's, but in attempting to "enforce" this later that morning I realized that it really wasn't my place to try and control the matter anymore. This was a welcome relief. Her capacity to engage with others would fluctuate unpredictably over the coming days and those who did come by to visit understood.

Our Daily Bread

E ach day at Elysian Hills begins with breakfast table conversation.

My dad and I checked in every morning with the process, discussing the practical whats and hows of the emerging strategy for supporting Mary Lou's journey and sometimes exploring the whys of what we were doing. These conversations challenged us each to the core as basic tenets, commandments even, were thrown into question. Balancing the witnessing of a person dealing with genuine pain and suffering in the face of a pure desire to end all that by dying with the burden of the direct request for us both to support and even enable that outcome saw us confronting options, possible actions we could take that were in any other context horrific.

We openly considered choices to help things along for Mary Lou by drug overdose or holding a pillow over her face. My dad shared a story of a friend of his who, at his life partner's request, put a plastic bag over her head at the last. When the person dying is a consenting participant and happy for the help, was this homicide, I wondered? If we did anything like that, how would that leave things for me and Dad? Certainly different from it happening "naturally," but not decidedly better or worse, for how far does it have to go before simply bearing witness to the discomfort, pain, and suffering of dying makes one culpable anyway?

Many unanswerable questions like this became familiar parts of the scenery as this amazing journey unfolded. At this level of intensity, just skimming the surface of daily life without any sense of a mandate really wasn't possible. It seemed like perhaps every question is ultimately unanswerable. I could see how building a house of certainty of thought and sharing with others in unspoken pacts regarding literal interpretation of ideas like "thou shalt not kill" is to rob ourselves of a connection to spirit, to source, to the unknowable knowing present in every moment.

It was freeing, if not also disorienting, to let go of this way of being part of a society of morality reduced to prescribed rules, but I had to. It was too uncomfortable and felt too wrong to put this level of ethical rigidity in the face of what felt so raw and real.

What if our society had more capacity to incorporate the unknown? What if ethical fortitude was collectively based more on principles than commandments? What if we shared a deeper language for dancing with the truths that we all share but don't talk about?

Like I said. . . so many questions.

Angels Among Us

———

"Humans become angels on earth, not in heaven."
Paramahansa Yogananda

For me, I gain a measure of peace in knowing beyond belief that the energy of living is more expansive than just our objective understanding of our material world. Existentially, or spiritually, or philosophically, I don't really care to try and understand, but in these situations, I can only call these guides *angels*. When present to the process of death and renewal, seeing these forces of universal grace and love and generosity is the only way I can stay grounded and process what is actually happening. I'm reminded of a friend who paraphrased Socrates in sharing his guiding ethos in life: "All I know is that I know that I don't know, and that is all I know."

Direct contact and communication with these beings, if I can call them that, has been a private matter for me. I've come across many people who are more practiced in this and so far, that has been enough. These people show up for me whenever I need this level of insight and support, and I'm always elated when they do, because they usually occur immediately as friends on a soul level. The kind of people I can trust and confide in at times that require baring my soul to stay alive myself. Therapists, spiritual guides, mediums, or just dear friends are there like a guiding hand to reassure me as I navigate the steppingstones of true change. I'm comfortable living with more a sense of knowing than faith that we all really are One and exist in this big soup of energetic truth before, during, and after physical life.

As the forty-four final days of Mary Lou's 34,548 days (yes, I'm a counter. . .) in this life progressed, my experience was lifted by the presence of these angels and their songs of joy and stark offerings of simple truth every day. I mostly kept this channel of knowing close to my heart out of respect, I guess, in my interactions with my dad. While I could tell he wasn't altogether closed to these ideas, he had his own comfort level with talking about it. I guess I granted him his privacy in the matter, as this wasn't a time to be distracted by discussing anything conceptual.

Everyone has their own language for acknowledging these forces, from coincidence to divine guidance, and I was fine with just letting that be. I'm more comfortable allowing the energies of connection and relatedness to flow between words spoken as this is where they live anyway.

In the final weeks, however, one undeniable angel graced the stage as Jennifer, one of the hospice nurses tasked with Mary Lou as a patient.

Skilled in her craft, with a commitment and passion for caring beyond any medical training, Jennifer would arrive to assess where Mary Lou was in the process and offer prescriptive advice for what we could do to support the next weeks or days. She had been traversing the country taking on various stints of employment as a traveling nurse throughout the pandemic.

When visiting Mary Lou, she would sit with us and share stories of her personal experience awakening to a bigger world as a young adult and venturing away from her rural Georgia nest of upbringing. Her thick southern accent betrayed any idea we might have entertained that she was "from around here" and the feeling that some version of fate had brought us all together was comforting.

Jennifer was dependably direct and always respectful in her communication. She was generous yet clear with where her compassion started and stopped. She always gave us as much time as we needed and wanted. It felt like we were the center of her world when she was there. We learned later that Mary Lou was one of more than twenty patients assigned to Jennifer and two other hospice nurses serving the entirety of southeastern Vermont who were active in the process of dying in their homes. Beyond that, Jennifer's own father was on his deathbed, outside of her professional purview but entirely included in the huge heart of compassionate care she walked in the world with.

Here I was, deeply consumed with just one case of dying. Considering what her life was like, driving hundreds of miles each day to touch and support dozens of dying people each week with each cadre of supporters probably being left with the same sense that she existed just for them, was eye and heart opening. Knowing such a remarkable person existed affirmed that my own capacity for compassionate care must be far deeper than I could ever imagine. It was humbling to watch her carry out her charge with ultimate gratification and a complete lack of getting caught up in any apparent injustice in a system that was asking more of her than seemed even remotely sustainable.

At the very end, during what she probably knew was her last visit, the friendship that had grown from her genuine interest and care in listening to our stories about Elysian Hills as the heart of Mary Lou and Dad's life was palpable. Before she left for her next patient, I sat with Mary Lou while Dad took her on a tour of the property, driving around the fields of Christmas trees with stops to take in the view and share stories of how the stone trees and family cemetery came to be. Upon their return, as we were hugging goodbye and sharing contact information, I could tell that she loved opening herself to us in such an intimate and personal way. She had to, probably, to maintain her own sanity and emotional health while doing her job. For to remain professionally detached, while that would have been fine, would, for her, have left her depleted. Helping people help their loved ones die was how she lived best.

I have no other word than *angel* for Jennifer, as she shared with lightness and joy in helping Mary Lou die and Dad and me live.

Surrender and Grace

———

"Death is not a period, but a comma in the story of life."
Amos Traver

When approaching one's last breath with intention, what there is to do could be described as untying the knots of connection that hold one's life together with sensemaking and obligations of relationship. I see this now as a sort of relaxation of the web of one's life story being left by its author to live on through the fading echoes of second- and third-hand retelling. Growing as the ripples of one's influence on others changed them and contributed to a grand orchestration of life.

Somehow in death there is a shift in the primary source of energy around one's life story. When young and fully alive, there is a vibrant energy of possibility for crafting one's story and sharing it firsthand. It can be reinforced and repeated, reinvented and rewritten, or left unshared in the corners of secrecy and privacy.

Mary Lou had a strong motivation, which was shared with Dad, to tell the stories of her life while she could. And they did just that. Her relationships with longtime friends and new great grandchildren were enriched and deepened in both simple and profound ways as she shared with a commanding sense of purpose. She offered teachings about her past and how events and choices shaped her as a person, always with a sensitivity to giving the bounty of her life lessons over as a moral to the story or nugget of wisdom. During one visit with her daughter Camilla, she gave voice to the lullaby she had sung to her as a baby which hadn't been heard out loud in some seventy years and spoke of the love they held and shared.

Regardless of what may be so about the life of one's soul after death and its continued influence on the living, there is a shift when moving on from physical form where one relinquishes being the source for that story and any opportunity for its future integrity is passed along to memory and the generosity of others when created anew. When Mary Lou died, I would no longer hear her tell her story as "my life" but I could continue to listen for my version of that story in any echo of contemplation or conversation about what "her life" meant or stood for.

It seems that when one is present to their own near death, creativity and wonder take a back seat with life stories and legend and legacy become the framework for their persistence. The seductiveness of the idea that the meaning of one's life might thrive and grow positively and posthumously inspires care in attempting to design the future state of anything one might leave behind. Material matters of one's estate can be remote controlled from a trust or will created before death, providing clues for others to find retrospectively of any chance to really know why. Beyond money and things, however, the ripples of lasting legacy only emerge as they arise in the waters of others' lives, melding with so many other stories, other ripples, with waves of meaning becoming magnified in alignment or canceled in opposition across countless interactions and iterations.

As a casting of vision, the hope that bridges the limitations of one's stated reality with their rendering of a desired future broadcasts seeds of possibility for actions others could take. Whatever care and intention one does or doesn't bring to planning their legacy, when it arrives in the world later, it is more a creation by others. In any case, as with stories in general, the life force of their existence is in meaning more than fact.

As a telling of history, facts take a background role as the desired meaning or lesson making up the teller's lens of interpretation is applied like interpretive paint on a canvas of "truth." Strokes of perception related and received, sometimes taking a glorious central role, sometimes discounted in relegation to a minor background blur, or even only existing in not being there at all. As a memorial of honor or proud declaration of principle, a storyteller's display of passion polishes the offering to an admirable shine.

Mary Lou's understanding of all this, and her role in framing her living legacy, was apparent to me in the underlying intentions guiding her vision for her celebration-of-life event. She wanted to create an environment where anyone who knew her could be compelled to show up without burden and feel safe in sharing unfiltered truths about their experiences with her. She wanted people to hear stories of what others liked and admired about her, along with jokes and revelations of what they didn't like or found challenging. "I want people to share the good, the bad, and the ugly," she said.

In this way, she offered the epilogue to the book of Mary Lou as a blank page, surrendering its writing and telling to the act of creation her community would provide.

My therapist later reminded me of one distinction between biological life and one's existence in relationship to others. "There are some who say we die twice," he offered. "The first time when our physical body passes on, and the second when the last person who remembers us dies."

Giving over one's physical body to its natural decay and return to the earth is one thing, but surrendering our memories and dreams to live on through those we've touched in life is something else.

Self, Family, Community, Society, and the Oneness of It All

———

"In the end, we'll all become stories."
Margaret Atwood

When I was finishing my environmental studies degree at the University of Vermont, my beloved advisor Ian Worley presented a version of this continuum to me as concentric circles of identity. He was a professor of philosophy and one of those quirky guys loved by students and peers for his dedication to the craft of teaching and commitment to truth in living.

One morning when Mary Lou was still partaking in the conversation but without the eating, Dad and I were tasked with the planning of her end-of-life celebration. She had lists galore, but nonetheless finite ones, of things she wanted to tend to and wanted us to tend to before she died and after. Right down to being given a punch list of things to do around the house in the first forty-eight hours like changing out the curtains for the winter ones, washing and folding the summer ones in a specific way, along with other to-do's.

Regarding her celebration, this was something she had been actively planning for quite some time. There was an entire folder of information on the subject, dogeared from having been added to, revisited, and revised over years. It contained favorite quotes and jokes to be read, pictures, and a soundtrack of music selections carefully chosen and ordered to help set the tone and affirm Mary Lou's less expressible feelings about her life. The care and time she had put into designing her end-of-life celebration knowing that she wouldn't be there to host or produce the event made it one of the most important concerns for us all to discuss as we got ready to make it happen.

At the breakfast table that morning, we put pen to paper regarding dates, location, timing, weather considerations, menu design, who should be invited and not invited, and how and what the "run of show" would look like. Event planning and production are in my wheelhouse more than either of them probably knew, but I sensed she understood that more than I thought when her gaze caught mine like she was tossing me a ball with the question, "Who will be the emcee?" I'm not sure Dad noticed the handoff as he was understandably caught more in the tunnel vision of

"Is this really happening?" but I got it and said, "I would be honored to serve in that role." Done and decided. Check that off the list for her and add it to mine.

After tending to the primary concern for her experience and the obligation to include most family members in the "departure" process beforehand, her celebration would bring her community together in a more public way. I saw my task in the emcee role would be to facilitate a group sharing of remembrances and stories in such a way as to evoke a whole view of the rich tapestry of varied perspectives. This would be another way for me to steward her sendoff in the special way she wanted: to honor and include some of the bigger circles on this community continuum with authenticity and the grease that humor provides in naturally awkward social situations making it easier for people to show up, listen honestly, speak up, and find meaning.

As in the story of the wise people and the elephant, the essence of what makes us all parts of a singular oneness would be left hanging in the silences sprinkled throughout the spoken words. With each voice contributing its unique tone and style, Mary Lou would come alive again for each of us as we learned new things about her and became steeped in gratitude for all that she brought to so many along the way.

Stories, Legacy, and Transformation

———

"People forget facts, but they remember stories."
Joseph Campbell

So much of the sharing I participated in and witnessed as a small parade of people came and went from Mary Lou's bedside was the telling of stories. Some we had heard many times and some never before told. The unique sense of urgency and license to be heard that a person getting close to uttering their last words commands opened a beautiful channel to pass along the happenstance of her life's experience as a proxy for those who would, if they could, pick up and carry her spirit forward.

For Mary Lou, building a sense of assuredness in eternal life while letting go of it all once and for all seemed to be the task, and when it was my turn, I sat and listened like a little boy obedient and polite. Listening for the wisdom of an elder sharing something that at face value I could in many ways not care less about, yet entranced with reverence by the generosity of what was being offered for me to discover between the uttered words.

As I listened to the stories of Mary Lou's childhood and life and how they were related with the dual purpose of passing along lessons learned and offloading a catalog of historical accounting of a life lived, I wondered, "What is my obligation here?" It felt like finding myself a recipient of a dying person's desire to contribute their wisdom must come with some purpose. This focused my listening and as I stretched through layers of surface comprehension and acknowledgment that I was hearing her, nodding, and responding reflectively as a signal that she could let go when ready now that her stories were safely transferred, I noticed the glimmer of myself in the reflection of shared human experience.

Beneath the obvious and fascinating differences in the circumstances of a person whose identity was substantiated decades before I was born, I compared, in a way, what I have learned and may yet learn about myself and tried to notice opportunities to level up in the face of this gift of intimate sharing.

Much of what was related was a basic historical account. Then there was a layer of ego in regalement of accomplishments and contributions. For Mary Lou, I didn't feel she had much need to be rewarded on that level. Rather, it seemed she was spinning the yarns in a way to invoke a moral to the story, all carefully placed in a substrate of ethical affirmation. There was no questioning of right and wrong for Mary Lou, it seemed, just a careful process of scheming how best to invite and impart rightness on others.

Beyond advice, for Mary Lou was gracious enough to leave my growth to me, her sharing and Dad's fervor in underscoring the importance of the process while sharing his own versions of the accounts, felt more like a tap running until the water ran clear. I felt a sense of honor and maybe peace amidst an air of knowing that I wouldn't discover what, if anything, to "do" with this information any time soon.

I identified this sense of a weight of responsibility in carrying others' life stories forward as a big piece of the sense of burden or incompletion I see in the back of the eyes of people who have lost a loved one.

I also saw the way that transformation, the kind of personal evolution spurred by instantaneous insight or revelation that, once revealed, one cannot go back from, is a shared experience. Not at all the same for both involved, and with no need to understand or share it in the moment either, but more the beauty of granting an "allowing of change" together. Like lovers taking in a sunset together in silence have no need for words as they acknowledge the beauty of another day coming to a close with a gentle reach and soft holding of hands.

As the offering of stories and gift of listening were shared and received, nothing else was needed to complete the way this shared connection changed both Mary Lou's and my life. From the perspective of legacy, it was simple and clear. She would go on to stop sharing stories and I would go on, however changed in this moment, to continue sharing my own stories which couldn't not embody some reverberation of her essence.

Giving and Receiving

—

"Giving and receiving are different expressions of the
same flow of energy in the universe."
Deepak Chopra

Like attending some cosmic swap meet or distribution
center for the universe of things, along with all the
careful sorting and cataloging, I witnessed exchanges between Mary Lou and her visitors occurring with intention
and increasing urgency at an exhausting pace.

Whether the active transfer of a special bowl, eques-
trian trophy, antique cabinet, or photograph, having held
value for Mary Lou before and now, newly relieved of its
decades of collected dust, offered as memento or keepsake
to a grandchild or friend. Or an exchange of energy in stories told, songs sung, bursts of laughter, sweet tears, gentle embraces, or locked eyes in silent gazes. Or when Dad
would hand her a warm washcloth to give her the chance
to cleanse with comforting waves of embodied sensation

as she washed her face each morning or night. I witnessed a procession of basic acts of kindness elevated to the status of timeless ritual in their simple intimacy and precious expression of love.

Not just Mary Lou either. I was present to this ever-unfolding web of transference in casual conversations I had in the driveway with passing neighbors, or in the kitchen with the home nurses, or on the phone in near daily conversations with my wife, my stepsister Camilla, and others. The halo of reverence surrounding this event of Mary Lou's dying called me to seek and see sacred meaning wherever I could and to share it more directly and openly than I ever otherwise would. An obligation, not required by anyone but, for me, mandated by respect.

I was reminded of how the deaths of other family members had opened doors to the deepening of other relationships for me. The blossoming of a sweet brother/sister-level connection with my cousin through our shared experiences surrounding her father's dying. The many openings to be more active in sharing and receiving love with my sister when Mom died. These relationships had always held the potential for more profound and intimate expression which in the surface-focused flow of daily busyness were not granted emergence until somehow unlocked by a death, becoming now precious and unavoidable.

Having been blessed by so many of these experiences, I had grown to carry a measure of hope for this gift of new life in death to a point where, like a child eagerly anticipating Christmas morning, I wondered what would emerge as the wrapping paper was torn away each time someone close to me died. In this case, I welcomed the chance to watch for these opportunities to grow together in new ways with Dad. Together, as we shared in the dying of a family elder, the light of truths that probably would not otherwise have been expressed shed enough of the weight of misunderstanding and judgments we had been carrying for decades to return us to the freedom of sharing the simplicity of love without expectation.

As with presents exchanged, the joy in giving and receiving didn't always come with a reward that was fulfilling or fun in the moment. The sweater Mary Lou knit for me as a child wasn't the best Christmas present I ever received and I probably only wore it once, but it was created and given with an intention of love that made it special in all its unfashionable embarrassment and itchiness. As a kid, the love and kindness with which it was crafted and gifted wasn't so important or meaningful, but now I could appreciate the offering she had made to a new stepchild as acceptance of me as part of her family too now.

I could have accepted Mary Lou's request for my support in dying as simply an invitation to give. To show up and be of service. However, beyond any idea of quid pro quo or obligation, the sacred space of giving and receiving and receiving and giving, all as an indistinguishable exchange of purifying energy, was like some mutual baptism as we each proceeded with our own living and dying.

Like living and dying, the experience of giving and receiving is elevated when each is embraced without being at the expense of or need for the other. Two words for an entirely singular activity.

New Life Flashing Before Old Eyes

"There is a crack in everything,
that's how the light gets in."
Leonard Cohen

The shining gift of new possibility for relationship from our shared experience of Mary Lou's passing process was clearly the next chapter emerging for Dad and me. Our capacity to talk openly about things as father and son was supercharged in the presence of Mary Lou's life ending. The act of reviewing Mary Lou's life made it safer and easier for Dad and me to share stories of our separate and innermost lives that would probably never have been voiced, not given Mary Lou's decision.

With the power of license to see and speak truth emanating from Mary Lou's dying state, Dad and I boldly, and with compassion, came to know things about each other that erased long-held barriers of judgment and enlightened each of us with a view of who we had always been beyond any walls we may have erected over time.

"Did Mom know that you were going to leave the house that day before you sat with my sister and me at the kitchen table and informed us that you were separating and no longer would live with us?" I asked at the breakfast table one morning. "Had you told her yet?"

"No, I guess not," he replied.

This was a simple exchange that, in touching on my first experience, at nine years old, of total existential loss, hadn't even occurred as a possibility for all the trauma privately outlived and healing ground that had been covered in the forty-six years since. In that moment, I didn't feel judgment for my dad and was accepting, even grateful, that he didn't feel shame. We simply understood and accepted each other's experience for what it was.

In that instant, a tectonic shift of energy happened in our family constellation as I realized that any forgiveness due in the matter was owed to myself, not Dad. While nothing changed about all the things I had made up about my role in why and how he left and who my dad was in that moment for me and for him, just hearing what happened in his world obliterated decades of stories of injustice, victimhood, and wounding. While Dad and I had eventually built our own closeness as father and son, the impact of that experience and what I had made up about it had rippled in waves of disruption and creation through my life, inciting core qualities of my identity and sense of self, all for better and for worse. Now, in confirming the simple truth together that, yes, that happened, and no there wasn't any intent to harm or cause pain, and no it wasn't my fault, something opened between us that felt like a new level of trust, compassion, and acceptance. To have left those truths in the unspoken space between us would have been fine really, at this point, but to have shared them out loud was healing in ways I could not have imagined or wished for.

That conversation continued, leading to others, and we unpacked so much about those formative events of my childhood and his fatherhood. The lightness of freedom from wondering whether love was really there beneath all the bumbling decisions and actions of each of our best attempts at living a good life emerged like the sunshine of a new day. We stood together for the first time since 1974, as father and son, able to accept all that had been lost between us and all that had always been there.

I know Dad and I would probably never have gotten that chance to recover our shared love for each other together as adults in time to build a new relationship from that place, if ever, without the way that Mary Lou's dying had brought us together.

Dad and I now talk every Saturday and frequently more often. Among all the exchange of ideas, and working out of deeper concerns, new and old, we openly share gratitude for the gifts Mary Lou helped manifest. Having the chance to engage and express our love at this level for months at least now and hopefully years before his or my eventual death is such a blessing and now one of my most cherished activities.

Continuum

———

Mary Lou believed in reincarnation, and this formed one of the core pillars of her self-concept. Discussions involving her past lives and how they directly led her to her place and duty as a steward of Elysian Hills were commonplace whenever I visited. It was important to her and my dad to keep those stories front and center and, not being opposed to any of that, I enjoyed the literal interpretation and certainty with which she spoke of the matter.

Her relationship to the land she was certain she had lived on in at least two incarnations was nothing short of a love affair. Even though the ownership of the property had been transferred to another local farmer years earlier, it remains conserved in perpetuity, forever protected from development and any use that strays from its purpose as she saw it.

As a couple, Dad and Mary Lou worked the land together in quite a progressive way for the time and her leadership as a woman farmer in the sixties and seventies was in many ways groundbreaking on a societal level. After a years-long search for the right successor stewards to take over, which included trial runs with prospective couples living and working at Elysian Hills for years at a stretch, they conceded to sell the property outright.

Dad's facility with such contracts, given his work conserving farmland with the Vermont Land Trust, helped them navigate a change in ownership without risking any compromise or change in the farm's destiny. So the sale went through with a number of conditions including that they both were to live out their lives there and be buried in a family cemetery they had built on the land, which by now contained five graves of beloved dogs that had romped the fields of the farm and their hearts over the years.

"When we die, we're going to the dogs!" they liked to say.

Her sense of stewardship so superseded any concept of deed or ownership that the idea that the current lead farmer and employee of the new owner who lived on the property might be able to take over the mantle was unavoidably compelling for her. It was clear that this man was a hard worker and could be a caring steward and that such an opportunity might be a boon to a young couple, but he and his wife had never expressed such an interest. Perhaps the idea hadn't occurred to them or perhaps they just weren't interested. Further, the current owner already had plans to pass the property along within his family when his time came. Yet even though no one else was thinking or planning in this way, for Mary Lou, the concept that this young man might somehow come to buy the property from his boss became an active pursuit almost to the end.

None of the unlikely practicalities seemed to matter to Mary Lou. She carefully explored the new idea in her last conversations with this man and his wife to nurture any shared spark of interest she might be able to champion. Further, in a more practical yet theoretical way, she anticipated and seeded the conversations and negotiations that might be required with the present owner, lawyers, and Dad, should the idea move forward, even though she had no legal standing in the matter.

I was struck and impressed by the audacity in her thinking. Watching her choose to latch on to this emergent idea which was much more aspirational than practical or real at this stage and invest her limited energy and time at the very end of her life to the idea underscored the clarity with which she held her role and responsibility in guiding Elysian Hills' destiny. In all practical senses she had no right to even be thinking like this. But I also didn't feel that she was being selfish at all in exerting authority or control beyond her purview. She simply couldn't not pursue any possibility of having a hand in realizing her dream of handing the care of Elysian Hills over to someone she felt shared enough connection and determination to do right by its fundamental spirit. Even knowing that she would die before this idea even really began to gain traction, if it did, if her influence could make it possible, even inevitable, she would do anything she could. It was an indefensible "hail Mary Lou" pass lofted with all the focus, care, and precision she could muster.

These things and more were left to my dad, and me to an extent, to carry forward when she was no longer around to steer the ship. Whether it was the special peony along the back fence which was to go to her longtime massage therapist and friend, or the seasonal changing of the window curtains, which she hadn't been able to do herself for years, or finding someone to buy the hutch or "buffet" (the name she preferred for its better marketability) that had been in the living room for at least fifty years, it was all on paper, committed to lists that were handed off as layers of letting go settled in.

With anyone else, the quality could have easily been brushed off as compulsive and obsessive, if not annoying. But with Mary Lou, it was just how she was. Love it or hate it, she always did what she thought others should think was best for them. A unique puritanical brand of egocentric selflessness that wasn't always easy to be involved with but defined a woman determined to live a life of truth and humble contribution in the world. Untenable rigidity on the one hand and admirable strength on the other, only tempered in its delivery by an incongruous undertone of compassion.

In evidence of the care Mary Lou and my dad invested in their relationship was the design of their wedding, especially their vows. Co-written and basically following the familiar frame of sickness and health, better or worse, etc., they took pride in sharing with me, (via the scrapbook including the original documents from the event right down to the accounting of how much the napkins and everything else cost, of course!), their intentional design of the last line. Instead of "'til death do us part" or "for as long as we both shall live," their vows ended with the phrase "for as long as we both shall love."

I had probably heard of this many years ago and if so, would have found it a meaningful revelation of their thoughtful and rich love relationship. But now, against the backdrop impending event of an actual life/death transition, I realized that the simple turn of phrase provided each of them with a relief valve of sorts on having to face the act of leaving or being left as a totality. For better or worse, their marriage contract wasn't designed to expire upon death necessarily, and I think this served to calm the emotional waters as the process continued.

Mary Lou and Dad had a conversation in the final week where she said, "I don't want to leave you, but I have to go."

Dad replied, "I don't want you to leave me, but I know you have to go."

This exchange felt like a completion, and they both seemed satisfied in the shared affirmation of their love with a sentiment that turned the page more than closed the book on their relationship.

Witnessing these simple but not so little things, and many others, has always left me with a growing reverence for what it is to have such a clear sense of place and purpose in life. Knowing my dad has maintained such careful dedication to the meaning of how, where, and with whom he chose to live gave me a backdrop to consider the possibility of my coming to know these types of truths of identity for myself with such clarity.

I admired them and was even a little envious, feeling my own sense of inadequacy or at least immaturity in similar matters. I realized that I was newly inspired to seek and understand my own sense of self and place. Their example showed me that I too could accept my dharma for what it is and become more active in cultivating meaning through consistent dedication and doing what it takes to live my life with a sense of purpose.

Mary Lou and Dad designed their lives to unfold in the context of the bigger continuum of existence, and the bold agency with which they carried on, knowing their relatively temporary place, made the way Mary Lou had decided to die make even more sense.

Holy Union

———

Dwelling on my interpretation of Mary Lou's final message to Dad, a poem came through:

Leaving You

I was alive for being me
Yet without you there would have been no us as
    witness
My life is therefore more ours than mine

In my death, all that which is ours continues
New versions of the story of my past are yours to
    tell now
The continued realization of my purpose still lives
    as a future yet to be discovered
Always as ever unfolding without end

I could never have known the totality of my place
    in the world
But for our love, shared joy, pain, confusion, ecsta-
    sy, and frustrations
Together we each have been becoming
More than either ever could have been
And as long as anyone we've touched, or who
    they've touched is living
So shall we be alive as always we were

Now you can still be you
As always alone as we
With me still by your side

It Sounds Easy, Dying

——

Maybe the idea of dying, while given status as a big deal, sounds easy because it seems so definitive to be living or not living. While this may seem a simple occurrence of momentary change, nothing feels simple about all the moments leading up to and, in a completely different way, following death. As a biological process, dying doesn't happen in just one moment at all anyway, so why do we rush to collapse the chance for a death to unfold at its own pace into a singular moment with such ease? For me, understanding that dying "naturally" happens slowly on all levels alleviates much confusion in the experience of witnessing it.

On the surface, I can take solace in hearing that someone "died instantly," ergo "they didn't suffer" or at least for long. But after witnessing Mary Lou's extended final dying process, I don't think I would willingly opt to avoid any suffering I might feel near the end in favor of the chance to have the process unfold over time. Getting to soak in the richness of the experience and quality of sharing with others in a "reasonable" amount of time is not to be missed in my best estimation now. Suffering and then breaking through into new joy in being is, for me, a fact of life, so why would I short circuit that at the end?

I remember when my father-in-law was diagnosed with terminal cancer. I was sharing about the situation with a friend, and she asked, "How long does he have?" Upon my reply that the doctor had given him three months, her response surprised me. "Oh good," she said, "that's enough time for him to say goodbye but not so long as to invite undue suffering." Before then, I hadn't stopped to consider practicality of timing in terminal cases like that. I had been too focused on the sense of tragedy in anticipating the loss.

In this way, I've come to see the process of dying and one's relationship to it as no more easy than that of living. In the final hours and minutes, the prospect of living, in the more practical context of what opportunities might exist for one to "live for," becomes a very finite and eventually exhausted activity. One last chance to let go and surrender to just living begets the final breath and, not so paradoxically perhaps, the last thing to live for is to die.

"I can't believe this is happening," my mom said out loud about a week before she passed. "I want to die consciously," another friend said with about a month left. "I don't want to leave you, but I have to go," were among Mary Lou's final words to Dad.

I realize in writing this that I don't know how I want to die yet. Many times, I've imagined my possible demise, often via some unforeseen accident or what others would refer to as a tragic circumstance after the fact, usually gaining some perverse sense of peace in fantasizing about a sudden or at least unavoidable happenstance. Falling off a cliff, getting hit by a bus, going down with a broken airplane, getting mauled by a bear, or trampled by a female moose. Stuff like that. I've wondered what the experience might be like and what others, if there are any around me, might feel or be focused on. Probably all of us have fantasized about attending or watching our own funeral, and I guess I've lauded the idea of invoking the emotional escape hatch of "At least he died doing what he loved."

After contemplating Mary Lou's very thoroughly considered choices about her own dying, I see my own heretofore loose and general projections so far as stemming more from the urge to take care of others and how that focus sidesteps any real considerations for myself. How might I hold my relationships now such that when that time comes, however it does, others would be more able to smile, celebrate, and find peace and strength? How will I be holding my relationship with myself when the time comes? Will I be at peace with me? Or will I still be more focused on others? Could I be successful in turning up the brightness on the light of my living in the act and experience of dying?

I once navigated an emergency wilderness ordeal with my best friend, carefully minimizing risks and keeping our bodies moving forward toward the car as the sun set, with miles to cover from when he had lost consciousness and collapsed deep in a remote desert canyon. With no other humans in at least a fifty-mile radius and no way to communicate or get help, we were consumed with genuine concern for survival. We made it out and I only realized how close the possibility of his death had been when I learned the next day that, in the hospital, he had been diagnosed with renal failure. This was serious yet survivable enough in a hospital setting but certainly not had we been confronted with the worst of those symptoms in the middle of the night in the vast ocean of Utah desert.

My relationship with Rob changed out of that experience. No one saved anyone's life that day, but together we had survived another excursion. In our shared brush with the real possibility of death a deeper connection of trust and unspoken understanding took root. In practical terms he has become my go-to emergency contact and even back-up beneficiary in my financial world. While he wouldn't miss a beat in accepting my death, I relish the chance to discover what we would share with each other in the final weeks, given the chance.

So, my relationship with my own death has been informed by direct experience witnessing others, by distant thoughts or reading books, watching actors perform the act, etc. Also shaped by a maturity, if you can call it that, that has come from more intimate and real conversations with my parents and others confronting the closing chapters. These conversations have shown me that, at least in the case of a "natural" aging/dying process, when one is conscious, honest, and graceful, there is much to sort out and tend to. Mostly practical things at first, like the stuff of an advanced directive or committing wishes for the distribution or disposal of material items and money as legal instructions to a last will and testament. Even succumbing to preordering the services that the business of dealing with dead bodies offers, like reserving a burial plot, buying a casket, having a gravestone crafted, or paying in advance for cremation and funeral services.

Then there's another layer of thoughtfulness, stemming more from the spiritual and personal realms. Things like planning one's memorial or celebration service, writing the obituary, having real "dress rehearsal" conversations with those likely to be present or empowered by legal declaration/contract to make decisions when the dying one can no longer rationalize or communicate. In these types of conversations, I notice that so much is focused on how one doesn't want to die. But what of how you *do* want to die? These things, at least in my experience, seem to get much less attention. Perhaps because they're more about the qualities of living as one dies.

Mary Lou was crystal clear on a few main dealbreakers in this realm. She didn't want to ever end up in an "old folks' home," or to ever have life-sustaining care become status quo. She did want to die in her home at Elysian Hills. It would be a mostly private experience and while Dad (and I) could be there, she didn't want a cadre of family or other people around.

Given Mary Lou's calculated approach to decision-making and planning, I wondered about the relative weight she placed on the things she knew she didn't want vs. those she did. It seems easier to know when an idea doesn't feel right than to commit the added act of creativity involved in envisioning and declaring what one does want. How much might she have felt backed into a corner given the things she knew she didn't want, being a burden on Dad and others, having to go to a care facility and leave Elysian Hills, living without the ability to create things with her hands. Did the growing presence or risk of these undesirable things happening make her feel like she had no other choice? Or was she more forward facing in designing her own best experience of dying? Of course, to reduce all this to such a false dilemma cripples one's ability to perceive other possibilities and whatever she felt was at least a mix of "didn't wants" and "did wants."

More unanswerable questions well worth spending time with.

Beyond the circumstances of her actual dying and death experience, there were more clear enough sounding, but murky-to-execute, qualitative wishes. Not being in too much pain, not being a burden on others, having people not cry or wail in mourning but rather to celebrate the truth, "the good, the bad, and the ugly," of her life. Banning the color black at her celebration event. (Red was prescribed and other colors acceptable as long as they were bright and vibrant.)

The best Dad and I could do with these desires was to find ways to share them with others and recruit or enroll more of a group understanding and will to honor them. As with all best intentions, the things Mary Lou described could only point to a more unspoken energy she wanted those around her to feel underlying their own relationship to her as and after she died. It wasn't about the color of any mourner's clothing but more an invitation, expressed as an insistence, that people find a way to focus more on the energy of celebration than sadness.

I was grateful for this personally, for it affirmed how much Mary Lou had cultivated this type of positive attitude, as she called it, in living a life that brought her so much joy. Mandating that people not cry wasn't an act of control or blockage of feeling sadness, for her it was a way to support people in not missing out on also feeling the lightness and joy that celebrating a life well lived offered too.

On the most basic level, dying *is* easy. When the time comes, death just happens no matter what we may have said or done to arrange the circumstances or anticipate, accelerate, or stall the process. Considering the web of energy that makes up our conscious familial and social community of relationships, however, it's easy to make it more complicated than it probably deserves.

I now know what I really would love to feel in dying, if at all possible, is to know and be at peace with that I am done. It's probably all folly but I do fantasize that if I could possibly be consciously absolutely done with living, that would be the moment I die. In any case, now able to see beyond the martyrdom of making my dying more about how comfortable others can be with it, I can think more about how I would "love" to die for me.

However it goes, all I do know now is that death happens, and dying is just another chance to live today.

Service

An interesting authority is granted to one who is dying. How we become compelled to put another's needs first because, in all likelihood, this is their last chance and not ours. Like the way we offer silent presence to a grandparent or elder when we know they're sharing something important to them, even while we don't really find it relevant or important ourselves in the moment. It seems only respectful to defer my own needs when I'm with someone who is dying.

At the same time, I've noticed the highest respect I could summon also involves retaining my own responsibility to direct my experience. For to deny my innermost feelings and needs in favor of others is never anything less than depleting, exhausting, and unhealthy.

In this way, being with a dying person challenges me in its "call to being" where I would be disrespectful in not also honoring myself to the greatest extent I can. As someone whose dharma this go around has so far largely been about learning to care for myself, I've found that to honestly care for and love myself is the first and best thing I can do in support of others.

I now know love as a way of being rather than a transaction-based reward or sacrifice. The field of love is something to *be* in and from rather than *do* for or in order to. So given this rare chance to share the experience of Mary Lou's dying together, I also understand that my best life becomes my experience when I approach dying as an act of living and living as an act of dying. Not as esoteric as it sounds, I now find peace and joy in knowing that I am dying now and, while I may not actually experience death very soon at all, this gives me immense freedom in living toward my best death and dying from my best life.

Mary Lou's granting me a measure of authority in helping to facilitate her dying left me grateful to find myself in this position. It offered me another chance to better dance in decision and action with the subtleties of another's authority granted and my agency claimed.

So, in Mary Lou's situation, as it was rapidly becoming biologically too late to change her mind and reverse course, I saw overstated, if not even forced, reverence beginning to show up. The possibility for denial on all fronts melted into whatever form of grace those who came in contact with her could bring. Not that there was ever really any hint of her wavering, I still wondered what form of betrayal would arise should she back out? How would she and others feel in finding out that all those sincere, awkward, intimate, and careful final conversations were really just a dress rehearsal? How would they then be different when the "real" time came? Would there be forever something in the way? Did any of that matter?

Mary Lou was a master of cutting through complicated emotional situations with sheer will, making them straightforward and direct. The wisdom in this model for efficiency and confidence in living was another gift for me in having the honor of knowing her and one I'll probably (hopefully!) take a page from when my time to die shifts from future to soon.

It was a joy to feel a direct partnership with Mary Lou during this time. She knew I accepted her choice and had the capacity to make the tough decisions and do what it took to see her carry it out. I was honored, and beyond that, happy to shoulder that responsibility so she could be free from managing anything she didn't or couldn't want or need to.

My gift of service to both her and Dad was both a duty and a pleasure. Knowing that neither Mary Lou nor I would have arranged it any other way provided the energy to stay the course and make it happen along with all the good, the bad, and the beautiful of it.

Being of service. Giving unconditionally. Surrendering to another's needs. When done without sacrifice, i.e., with near equal attention on receiving as well, this way of being is a beautifully satisfying way to live and share love.

Time for a Popsicle

—

Of course popsicles are mostly water. That and, in the case of the ones Mary Lou was enjoying, also twenty-seven calories worth of energy each. Certainly not enough to live on long term but I was concerned about how much even that level of sustenance would prolong the process.

When I first arrived, my concern about the popsicles was more focused on what seemed antithetical to her declaration. I wondered what may be involved with what I saw as a lack of rigor and integrity with respect to the difference between what she had declared and what she was doing. Was it ignorance? Was it weakness? Was it a sign of perilous ambiguity? Did the fact that she and Dad maintained that she wasn't eating or drinking yet she was eating four or more popsicles a day belie a situation that would cascade into failure later on in the process?

I didn't want to become the popsicle police and, at least for starters, stowed my conflict in favor of support for the immediate benefits they provided. Being able to still engage in the act of eating along with the oral stimulation they afforded tempered the adjustment to stopping eating all other food. In the first week before I arrived, while she had begun her final fast, with the popsicles, she could continue the familiar routine of joining Dad at mealtime and ease the awkwardness of going out to eat with family at their favorite restaurant which had been an important regular (monthly or so) event for many years.

As a child, she had enjoyed the frozen treat and so her delight in having a license to eat nothing but popsicles all the time introduced an energy of fun and devious satisfaction. I couldn't call it a "last supper" per se, but some of that idea of having the last thing one eats be among their most cherished foods was there.

She rotated among three flavors and made up each as a proxy for real foods she used to enjoy calling the morning orange one "orange juice" for breakfast, then "salad" for lunch came in the green variety, and for supper the red one signified "lobster," which she had always immensely enjoyed indulging in on their vacations to the shore.

As the next couple of weeks unfolded, I observed that, to whatever extent having some water and sugar each day extended her period of lucidity and energy, it was supporting her ability to interact with visitors which was also clearly very positive.

Increasingly, I was compelled to keep the issue top of mind as I anticipated that when it came time to cut back on and stop eating popsicles too it would have to be an act of willful abstinence. With Dad and Mary Lou separately, I talked about how they were serving to keep her alive and kept putting questions in front of them like "What's the goal here?" and "How long do you want this to take?" I wasn't being pushy as much as seeking genuine understanding in my confusion at how best to support given what she said she was doing wasn't entirely lined up with what she was actually doing.

With a combination of somewhat reluctant willpower and mutual agreement among the three of us, the tide shifted and what had started as four or five a day became three, then just one. I think this was mostly affirming for her as to be in control, even if it wasn't fun, helped her feel and know that the process was succeeding.

When approaching what was the apex of her most conscious pain in the process, the conflict became more explicit. She was growing increasingly distraught that the process was taking so long, and the popsicles stopped all together, then also water. As her body became dehydrated, she became highly agitated and delirious begging and pleading for water or ice, sucking on the wet face cloth, and getting quite upset. Dad and I hated this but thought it must be the time to tough it out and force death's hand. It was difficult to coach Camilla when she came to sit with Mary Lou and give Dad and me a break that even though her mom would likely ask, even plead for water and possibly resort to deception and lying to get it from her, she had to not give her any.

We really didn't want to be doing this as it did feel wrong. Thankfully, we would soon realize that taking the idea of not drinking literally and disallowing any water as much as possible had pushed things too far. This came from reviewing our challenge with the hospice nurse, where we learned that the body's drive to stay hydrated was beyond physical. The urge is so primal and strong as to resort to even self-deception or delusion in getting water in absolutely any way possible. Lila, the lead hospice nurse, told us that she had never seen nor heard of anyone being successful in willfully dying of dehydration. She related that in caring for terminal patients, this desire for water would stop on its own, but only very near the end (hours or maybe a day), when kidney and organ failure was imminent. She went on to share that, as a medical professional, to deny someone water was so much in conflict with the goals of palliative care as to be inhumane and that, in a hospital setting, no doctor worth their salt would withhold water.

This was all so very good to know, and I wish I had the benefit of this understanding sooner as we likely could have avoided much strife and only at the more than well worth it cost of a couple more days, maybe.

At that point we shifted to leaving ice chips by her bed in a bowl and allowing her to self-regulate, having as much or as little as she wanted.

While personally I'm not inclined to abdicate much authority to a doctor just because they have a license, taking on the responsibility of care in a home setting was daunting for my relative lack of knowledge, training, and experience in the medical realm. Sure, there were the guiding voices and direction, even mentorship, of visiting nurses, but there were so many moments, in the middle of the night, or when a medical expert was unavailable, when common sense came up short and Dad and I had to do our best and hope we were getting it right.

I'm a strong advocate for home health and undergoing hospice care outside a hospital or skilled-care facility setting and can't emphasize enough how developing a candid and open relationship with a trusted medical expert is one of the most valuable and empowering things anyone in a supporting role can do.

Digging Deeper

———

"Maybe death isn't darkness, after all, but so much light
wrapping itself around us – as soft as feathers."
Mary Oliver

Reviewing the list of individual deaths I'd had the honor and onus to experience over the previous year I saw that, if the opportunity to be renewed by new life through other relationships growing to overflow any hole left by the passing of another was somehow a universal law of balance, many of these gifts were more subtle, if not imperceptible altogether.

Conspicuous or not, I like to believe that a gift is always exchanged, for this seems the nature of life. I also see that being aware of it seems a rare occurrence out of which I can actively cultivate understanding and meaning . . . or not. Applying this mix of surrender and intention has become a reliable catalyst for serendipitous new joy arriving to temper lasting emptiness with fresh gratitude. In any case, this belief gives me grounding.

In this case, the extended experience of holding space for Mary Lou and Dad and being in this massive open field of exchange continued. I felt my capacity to be present was being challenged to the limits of my physical/emotional capacity to give and receive. As the days ticked by into weeks beyond any expectations we all had for how long this would take, Dad and I grew tired. Unable to sleep with a level of restorative unconsciousness, and as our bodies and minds loosened under the exertion, a timeless liminal state came to predominate. Curiously, at the same time, like sunlight finding a path through passing clouds, more and more energy would become available, and we discovered new reserves of capacity to continue. We had to.

As an ultra-marathon runner, I know how to pace myself. Monitoring and managing my energy over dozens of hours and scores of miles. Leaning in and accelerating when the inner and outer terrain align and I feel the urge and desire to run and slowing my gait when feeling depleted. Taking care to not stop except briefly at an aid station or particularly inviting resting place to refuel my body and collect my psychological energy for continued forward movement toward the finish line.

This training helped me in this different version of endurance experience. I trusted that regardless of what I thought I was capable of, my body and spirit would surprise and reward me with unknown new reserves of strength just as I needed them and often just after I thought I couldn't possibly continue.

Self-care took the form of breaks. I took myself on walks, went on short runs, got in the car to go get a sandwich from Subway, or drove a few dozen of the many miles of Vermont dirt roads through corridors of colored fall leaves with no destination in mind. Never letting go completely, but allowing my mind to wander, having handed off the job of active support for thirty to sixty minutes or so at a time.

Sleeping was also mostly a conscious exercise as it was nearly impossible to "turn off" my awareness enough to fully rest despite my body's exhaustion. I sat in bed and did crossword puzzles or watched a movie on my laptop until one or two in the morning when I would basically pass out for a few uninterrupted hours, if lucky, always with one ear on the rest of the house, listening for any need to arise regarding care for Mary Lou or Dad. While some of this sleep was, according to the clock, blissfully deep, my dreams were highly active. They offered a bizarre profusion of liminal images, feelings, metaphors, and meaning, the content of which began to blend and blur with the daytime reality of each waking moment.

Daily life became a fluid shifting from half-awake to half-asleep with a rhythm like tides ebbing and flowing, or the moon waxing and waning with its longer monthly cycle, or the changing season from late summer to early winter, or, of course, the beating heart rhythm of radiance as the sun was setting on a ninety-five-year-long life.

The Will to Live

———

It makes sense that sooner or later many people find answering the question of "What do I have to live for?" important or even imperative. This exercise of identifying what I'll call meaningful attachments is probably healthy to engage in at any point in life. Knowing one's purpose, even if temporary or obvious, gives us a canvas on which to paint the stories of our lives through our choices, actions, accomplishments, and failures.

All the while though as we're playing with this tug and pull of purposeful living and living fully, we seem to take the living state of our body for granted. Biologically designed to survive, for the most part our physical body can withstand great harm and injury, heal itself, and go on living for an expected eighty to 100 years or so. Of course, there are exceptional influences that shorten or lengthen that time but, on the whole, most of our living days, our physical lives are highly dependable. We've grown comfortable with a sureness that we'll still be around tomorrow to continue our journey. Life and death level threats to our physical wellbeing and crises of a more metaphysical nature, like that of losing and finding purpose, are different things yet related.

As the more than month-long process with Mary Lou, Dad, and me holding the space for her dying unfolded, the realities of the gap between her body's will to live and her mind's will to die presented challenges that were mostly very painful to witness.

Hearing her increasingly desperate pleas to have it be over now and be done with the pain of physical living, while seeing her body continue finding ways to thwart her desires and survive another hour, another day, felt nothing less than cruel. Beyond any control, given our commitment to a largely "natural" or at least unassisted death on a physical level, I struggled to make satisfactory meaning out of what the universe (my name for a higher power) was dishing out for her. What more was there possibly to learn? Was there something else left to say? Was there something we were subconsciously doing that might be keeping her here?

It was oddly almost a relief to be too exhausted to dwell or ruminate on such questions as I tend to do. To hang in there and do my best to be at peace with my drive to resolve urgent questions falling flat, leaving them unanswerable in the face of what was happening, brought up a fear that I couldn't follow through, that I might reach my own limit and fail in noticing the next opportunity to serve. Being committed to not sacrificing or martyring myself was in conflict with the expression of love and care I was also committed to. But worrying more about me also felt arrogantly selfish given that whatever she was going through in the minutes and hours of lying in wait, coming in and out of consciousness, was surely an experience of pain that I couldn't fathom.

Mary Lou always had a clear set of ideas about why she was living and what was left to accomplish. At the top of the list was preserving the sanctity and existence of Elysian Hills' highest expression as she saw it, passing along any and all salient wisdom that she had collected to those who could carry on the mantle of stewardship. That and, of course, honoring the sanctuary of sharing the ups and downs of daily life with her beloved husband, business partner, and friend, my dad.

As her dance with these "drivers" of purpose evolved with age and her bucket list grew short she became motivated to also leave her life of things behind as gracefully as possible. For her, that involved a determination to get rid of her stuff, the physical items that she had collected and enjoyed throughout her life. She took this project on with typically almost excessive fervor beginning at least ten years before she passed.

After heirloom-level items were tagged for surviving family members, the antique furniture went to auction.

Then, many other items were collected and became the ulterior impetus for a family and friends gathering they called "The Schmidt Bash." This family reunion-style event, along with the goal of sharing quality time late in life with family and friends, was all about having guests leave with items that were hopefully meaningful for them.

A ritualized transfer of the wealth of meaning encapsulated in stuff.

Humorously, there was one item displayed on the set of large tables in the back of the room, some sort of wooden farmhand tool that no one, including Dad and Mary Lou, could identify for its use. And Kathy and I still have an interesting collection of old colored glass bottles on display over our kitchen cabinets that we "won" the right to bring home after one of the party games at the Bash.

I remembered a mildly heated conversation one morning at the breakfast table five months before she made her decision about the peony visible from the dining room table. Mary Lou had just asked me to help Dad dig it up and bring it to a friend who she had decided could enjoy and care for it after she died. Dad, feeling his place in the matter usurped, shared that he wasn't done enjoying it yet. After Mary Lou conceded that she was afraid that no one would do it after she wasn't around anymore, I promised her that I would not let that happen and the peony project was relegated to the list of things to do when Mary Lou died.

Standing back, the whole process of clearing stuff, which I observed and sometimes helped with over the years, had an air of part bequeathal of heirlooms and part yard sale. I appreciate the value of not burdening surviving heirs with a mountain of things to wonder how and what to do with and have adopted a smaller version of this practice for myself already as I try my best to turn the tide in my life of things from inflow to outflow.

So, about nine or so years after the Bash, when Mary Lou got to making her decision to die, her load was admirably light and her list of "reasons to live" had been shortened essentially to her most heartfelt joy in living, her marriage. I don't know how long she considered the many factors in what the act of dying before Dad involved but, they had been discussing this likely scenario in general terms for more than a couple decades.

While I've mentioned the specificity of her last lists of tidying up life's chores that we helped with in the final month, the piece about leaving Dad physically without leaving the marriage energetically remained increasingly elevated and held with calculated care. She had been keeping track of what her physical existence meant and made possible in their relationship as qualities of life-sustaining joy on one side and burdensome onus for Dad on the other. The balance continued to shift as her own experience of diminishing physical capacity forced her to stop farming, cooking, quilting, working at her computer and desk, and finally needlepoint. Thus, when the scales of her assessment tipped in favor of paradoxical certainty that her commitment to bringing joy to their marriage would be better served by not being here, the decision was finally clear as more mandate than choice.

Mary Lou liked reaching obvious-feeling solutions to challenging situations and whether her certainty on a mental level or her surrender to the inevitable came first or not, the choice became unavoidable, and she mustered the strength to follow through. Instead of focusing on her lack of things to live for, she chose to consciously create all she had to die for.

I got it and was truly awestruck. Honestly, I'm not sure I could do that.

Unfinished Stories

———

Grant me the serenity to accept the things
I cannot change, courage to change the things I can,
and wisdom to know the difference.
The Serenity Prayer

As attentive and careful as Mary Lou was to tie things up, completing her lists before she moved on, there were things she left arguably unaddressed. That assessment bears finer distinction because for her, as I understand it, the broken relationship with her youngest son was something she was at peace with as far as anything she was called to "do" about it. So, her adamance in recruiting the rest of the family's alignment in not informing him of her decision to die intentionally or including him in the process in any way, while uncomfortable for me, was a simple matter to honor.

For my own sake of peace, I had to be careful in not colluding with her story about how he betrayed her and what that meant and, perhaps mostly as I really had little to do with him in my life so far, it was not that difficult to set aside any sense of wanting to try and instigate healing for them. The scope of the channel the river her life was flowing in now was vast enough to allow this point of pain to remain in the past, where she had already found the strength to leave it.

As sad or wrong as it seemed to me to not try and heal a family relationship and declare its broken state finished, Mary Lou had made it clear this was her wish. Clear on what she could control as well as what she was powerless to change, and accepting things as they were even though she probably didn't like it, was a display of more personal strength and surrender than I so far have ever known.

In the case of her son, to the extent that Mary Lou was matriarch, whatever judgment she was both accepting of and unwilling or unable to dissolve and transform was hers to die with. While the rest of the family each had to find their own peace with the state of this relationship when she died, at least she had the grace to be clear that the matter was decided and finished for her. If there was anything for any of us to do with that situation, that was our business, and she didn't want or need us to include her anymore. Relegated mostly to the unspoken in her presence, this story remained very much alive, at least for Dad, Camilla, and me.

Camilla couldn't accept her mom's request to exclude her brother for her own value of their sibling relationship and commitment to family. She could accept what was so for Mary Lou but couldn't collude and adopt the same position for herself. She resolved this by going ahead and connecting with her brother privately and sharing about their mom's decision and pending death.

A tenuous web of family secrets began to form, and I found myself in the familiar role of confidant for all parties landing me in my own catch 22 of impossible choices between promises, morals, and my own commitment to truth. I brought patience to the table in careful conversations with Camilla and Dad in particular, as each of them confided their own challenges around Mary Lou's demand to exclude her son and how that made each of them feel. I had some trepidation anticipating having to at some point make a choice between betraying Camilla's confidence in me or committing the secret to my own vault of buried truths, compromising my own emotional health, and building a wall that would put me in a position of being untruthful with Dad. I have mastery in the area of keeping confidences from my consulting work and being responsible with sensitive and proprietary corporate information, and on a personal level from myriad experiences in the role of "father confessor" (as my high school soccer coach named me once), as well as my years as a recovering alcoholic maintaining the sanctity of the AA community's pillar of personal anonymity. So, I don't know why anything would be different in this case, except that the way personal and family values overlap for me would make any decision to reveal or hide what I knew more difficult without feeling like I was damaging one or more of the three relationships I was committed to with Camilla, Dad, and myself.

Such are the seeds of family drama, and owing to the context of deep truth present in our journey with Mary Lou in her dying, I knew I would be able to be clear when the time came and could live with any outcome as long as I said my piece with a full heart in the moment.

In the end, after Mary Lou had died, Dad shared with me his considerable angst around how to communicate the fact to her son. At that point, I went to Camilla privately and shared my discomfort, letting her know that in my mind she had a choice whether and when to let Dad know she had betrayed the request. I let her know I would love her whatever she chose but hoped that she might find the strength to tell Dad sooner rather than later. I was clear that my biggest joy was in seeing how her relationships with both me and Dad (and her mom) had been entranced with so much light and love during the past month. That was all I could share. The rest was up to her.

Thankfully, she chose to come clean with Dad about her conversations with her brother and while there was certainly some strife for a few days, we were all able to reach peace and understanding with the hows and whys, and to my knowledge, no grudges were formed. I was happy to feel that the best opportunities for clear and honest future relationships were left for each of us to enjoy, or not, together.

Putting one's house in order after all is as much about finding a final resting place for the messy stuff as it is organizing and polishing the altar of our most cherished accomplishments for posterity. I doubt anyone goes to the grave without at least some baggage, and it was affirming to see at least Dad, Camilla, and me choosing to not add to ours over this.

Mary Lou may have had disappointments, but by the end it seemed, I like to think at least, that she had shed any need to place blame for things that didn't go her way on others or herself and could let go of any desire or need to do more. All was well.

I realized again how much I'd spent my life so far worrying about what others think, thus trying to corral a perception that favored my opinions while secretly continuing to promote my fears. Coming to accept that a mother can die in peace with the possibility that her love for her son may never resurface is difficult to be settled with but witnessing the faint smile on Mary Lou's dead face gave me a measure of strength in allowing others to do their thing without it being a threat to me even when that comes with pain. Mary Lou helped me come to know that our stories can be both done and unfinished at the same time. Moreover, perhaps that is the only way they even ever exist at all.

Along with our shared lives as a tapestry of stories interwoven as a relatively static display of what happened and what each of us made up about it, I wonder now if it's unfair to place judgment on which stories are good or bad, heroic or tragic, complete or incomplete. Of course, it's satisfying when love is present and the intersection of shared stories align in a sense of the experience being positive. We all love agreement. But stories are fluid in their ultimately fabricated nature and never really complete. At best they lead to what's further along the way whether rehashed, unraveled and rewritten to better satisfaction, or just ended as is, either way leaving the possibility of fresh new stories to begin.

So like leaves having finished their role of synthesizing light as a small part of the living system of a tree falling to rest on the ground, perhaps even our most persistent stories also break loose and transform in their purpose when we die, becoming layers of humus ready for new life. No longer vibrant and alive or connected to our living authority to edit or retell anew, they remain present even if in a natural state of decay as they continue to contain both past and future potential through their retelling at the hand of others.

Standing back enough, it's all just one story, as the leaf is connected to all trees, all forests, all fungi, dirt, and rocks. Even as its brief period of vibrant green seems the epitome of life, the nearly unfathomable power of its shared singular existence as the whole of all things resolves and dissolves urges to prolong its living state, preserve its beauty, or even deem it gone and discarded.

Different from legacy, the more subtle space of unspoken stories complete yet unfinished yields a new life force that transcends the passing of the author.

Last Conversations

The truth is that each time we share a conversation with another it could be the last.

Having strived for a number of years now to live with this as an active source of intimacy with many of the people I relate to, it seems odd that I spent so much time earlier in life stepping over the only opportunity we ever have to share fully, which is here and now. Being able to express this now brings me a sense of peace as the matter-of-factness about it wasn't this comfortable for a long while. It's taken time.

When I learned of Mary Lou's decision I didn't know if we would get another chance to share a conversation. I wrote her the email I shared earlier in case she was still around and able to read it but with awareness of the possibility that maybe she wouldn't even see it in the background.

Given that the time for any direct conversation was now decidedly finite, each one we got to have after that email held the poignance of possibly being the last. I'm not saying we shared a repetitive chorus of tearful goodbyes at all. Many times, our interactions were purely transactional regarding her or my needs in the moment, but the more mundane passing words exchanged so often in our daily existence were fewer and bringing care to sensing and saying anything that came up to be said now was important and seemed appropriate to do my best at.

Near the end, in the last week or so, I awoke each day with the question of whether there would be another conversation or not. We had said what needed to be said and I was settled with that we might be done. Our stream was running clear of things left unsaid at least for now and any new chance to add to the living exchange of our spoken and heard relationship would reveal itself like new rocks to be washed over downstream, until it didn't.

That Mary Lou "stuck around" longer than any of us anticipated offered more chances to have that last conversation for everyone in her life at that point and this was a curiously profound yet undramatic blessing. I called her middle son at one point who was a few hours away on a brief vacation with his wife to relate that his mom had been asking, "Where's [my son]? When is he coming back?" earlier that day and his initial response was "She's still here?" It wasn't at all a cold or uncaring comment, and I understood his momentary confusion as we were all growing quite amazed at her tenacity. He went on to say, "I've already said my goodbyes" and something like "Do I really have to come back?" Again, I heard and completely understood the practicality of how dropping everything to make time for more last conversations is another thing to fit into our busy schedules and dismissed any urge to answer that question for him. He did come back, after his time away, already complete yet open to more.

Witnessing this underscored how I sometimes gird myself against any potential pain of realizing something is now actually dead by what amounts to rehearsing it beforehand. To declare completeness and then have reality prove that declaration wrong is its own challenge but maybe easier to live with than holding on to hope for more beyond what bears out.

The dance between not wanting to let go and wanting to be done is private and personal with potentially many layers of emotional turbulence to be settled. But the fact always is that each conversation could be the last.

Okay then, so what? Such facts are meaningless until we bring meaning, subconsciously or with intention. So what do I choose to do now, knowing this could be it?

I remember the abject abyss of helplessness I felt when sitting with a friend some twenty years ago. She was numb with shock and disbelief in the onset of grief for having just learned that her oldest daughter of sixteen had died entirely unexpectedly of a sudden heart attack in home room at school that day. With that experience in mind, I'm liable to choose to cling unnecessarily but for-givably in response to the fear of losing someone closest to me before I feel ready.

On another hand, I remembered feeling compassion with an air of forbidden pity for another friend whose life of active meaning through job, hobby, and other daily coun-terpoints of creativity had been all but stopped for more than a year while her mother lay alive but unresponsive in long-term care. Witnessing this burden of sacrifice, I could see heroism, but it also made me sad.

This perspective made it easier to assuage my proneness to guilt in living for me by doing things that fed my soul even if it might mean leaving a loved one alone to die.

Realizing that each situation is different, it's clear there is no "right" choice along that spectrum that applies universally. Only the chance to cultivate a presence of mind to check in with myself in every, or more realistically some, conversations, and choose what feels right in my heart and then live with it.

Saying "I love you" to my wife before she left for work, if only in case my irrational worry-born visions of a deadly car crash were fated to come true that day, felt weak and selfish if done as insurance for not having to live with that I didn't share my love before she left. If simply a rote exer-cise, it felt cheap and undermining of how deeply I might have really meant it. I see now that what we feel and what we say or don't say are just two channels, one inner and one outer, for expressing ourselves each moment.

What matters more than sentiment is authenticity.

If I or the person I'm talking to were to die now or soon, what would I want my last words to have been? What might their last words have been to me? These are worthy questions but not ones to dwell on for too long, I think. Holding the energy of presence that these questions arise from is more of a practice or access point to simply becoming present. So at least for now, for me, this is the only answer to the "So what?" Strive to be present now and choose, without judgment, projection, or worry, what to say next. Then live with that.

Ready?. . . Set?. . .

———

Planning is essential.
Plans are meaningless.
Winston Churchill

What of the dance between how we want it to go and how it actually goes?

As Mary Lou approached her moment of transition, the paradox of seeing a person confidently and courageously moving actively toward an event that couldn't be controlled by her or anyone was a source of dynamic tension as we tended to our best efforts to support the process.

My role as an enabler was to go beyond, to see a bigger picture, and discover opportunities to contribute practical yet profound offerings.

"Dad," I said over breakfast one morning, "I know you're resistant to wearing your hearing aids and I'm not here to change that but let me ask you a question. When

Mary Lou speaks her last words to you, do you really want to be left wondering what she really said? Further, do you want her experience of your last word to her to be 'WHAT???'" In these small ways, I felt compelled to try and realign energies like stubbornness and compassion, or at least point out opportunities.

Dad started wearing his hearing aids again around her.

How, I wondered, would it go when the moment came? What level of consciousness would she be able to maintain as a participant/witness of the event? Would my dad be able to "be" there? And with what capacity?

We anticipate a death like something that will happen in an instant. One moment they're there and the next not. Even physically, I haven't ever seen this to be true. While choosing the moment of death might be a fantasy that if realized would seem to affirm some elevated relationship with the divine, to focus on this seems to me more an act of ego. Even writing these words feels blasphemous. Perhaps to call this folly is too simple. But really, when a death occurs, that's that. The chance to be present to it, whether you're the one dying or bearing witness to the happening, is as fleeting as the impossibility of truly being present anyhow.

I can't say any of this with much authority as I haven't experienced actual death myself, but being in a position of guide, partner, steward, coach, gatekeeper, witness, enabler, or whatever I could call it, with Mary Lou and so many others, I've only come to know the event as a washing over. More like the fluid shift between an in breath and an out breath. A moment where life is not even just possible but real and beginning yet again, and then all there is to notice is that that truth is no longer there.

But what of control? It's true, each of us has the power and ability to take actions that actually end our lives or that of another. But when it comes to it, when the reaper harvests a soul, or the angels escort a being from the confines of physical existence with radiant benevolence (equally odd concepts if you ask me...) isn't the best we've willfully done only to have invited the inevitable?

The only control we could actually exert seems to be with regards to timing. But still, when the transition occurs time seems irrelevant, there is no control and no recourse. The circularity of such wonderings is fodder for theological belief where there is nothing logical about it, yet the presence of order can only be attributed to something bigger than ourselves.

She was ready. Was I? Were we? Everything within our control and sense of responsibility was set. So what do we do now?

I would feel the eternity of time slowing in anticipation, with all senses attuned to the inevitability of an expected next moment, like being in a car crash just before and as it's happening or waiting for the bang of a starting gun authorizing sprinters to explode from the blocks.

These moments of waiting saw my attention continually focused on the pauseless transition from in breath to out breath. I sat with Mary Lou, wishing, hoping, and conjuring an impossible will to see her go now. I held my own breath, desperately wanting to feel whatever relief, onset of grief, joy, or sorrow, it didn't matter what, that would follow knowing that she had gone.

And, as that didn't happen, I would exhale and continue breathing with her, conceding another timeless moment of life in hopes of death.

The Brutality of Truth

—

I hadn't anticipated how harsh certain moments felt along the way. Fortunately, the totality of my life experience enabled me to be somewhat inured to the pain compassion dished up for me when Mary Lou just couldn't stand how much her physical body hurt in the face of how badly she wanted to be done and gone. As she wailed with the pain of her right leg, I did everything I could to help. She was angry and had reached a point where we were powerless to relieve her struggle to any remotely satisfactory level.

There was nothing she could do herself. Sheer will was no longer sufficient. Her body's default state of supporting its own living couldn't be overridden by want alone. She begged for help from a place beyond the capacity or desire to reason.

This presented my dad and me with conundrums impossible to play out to any acceptable conclusion with respect to the suffering we were all experiencing. I realized that when down to it, this reality, these exact moments, are what dredges confusion resulting from fixed interpretations of legal responsibility, ethical or liability concerns, and family dynamics.

None of us wanted to see her live or die in pain. The morphine helped at least partially in that regard in making it so she could slip seemingly, hopefully blissfully into deeper incoherence and some version of sleep. Regardless of any idea that this might be an unfortunate veiling of consciousness in the process, the sense of peace and being relieved from witnessing someone in excruciating pain at least for a few hours was welcome. It seemed that being alive and awake had become impossibly uncomfortable. We had reached another level where providing the best care we could meant letting go more and wondering if there would be any chance for peaceful, pain-free, conscious, two-way sharing again.

Act 39, Vermont's Death with Dignity legislation, seemed like it could be an option, given its intention to assist people who are clear in their own mind that they want to invoke a process that causes their death with as much haste and grace as possible. This seemed to suit Mary Lou's steadfast and conscious alignment with that purpose. However, the legal dance with culpability and liability had shaped the policy in ways that made it impossible for someone like Mary Lou to employ it. Not fitting their definition of *terminal* when she originally made her decision, she was not qualified to avail herself of Act 39. Then, by the time she did meet the requirements, she was too far along in her dying journey to be able to navigate the three-to-six-week process and take advantage of its offer of aid in dying by choice. It was disappointing to feel failed by the system in this way, but we understood how designing policies for the masses inevitably fails in some individual circumstances.

There we were.

The next home health aide visit was in two days when we would get some assistance with basic care and hygiene. The next visit from the hospice nurse was in three days. The last assessment was that she would likely live at least another ten days. Our only remotely effectual tools were pharmaceutical, and the morphine, lorazepam, and haloperidol were challenging to administer, but helpful enough with the pain management and anxiety to afford her some sleep, if you could call it that anymore.

Her pain was explicit and real. Our pain was private and personal, taking a backseat to the primary process in many ways. Unwilling to commit any act of intentional assistance and unable to get any immediate assistance from a medical professional, all we could do was fumble along with the ever-changing landscape of how to use the feeble tools we had to maximum positive effect. We were left to react as quickly as possible to the emergent and urgent need for any measure of relief she sought, while sitting in witness of a loved one's willful and sacred decision having invited unimaginable pain and suffering. Not fun.

If grace has a cruel side, this was it.

My only access to peace was through repeatedly letting go myself and just being present. A profoundly, I guess you could call it spiritual, clear, and simple, place of reverence for me far beyond constructs like faith and trust or beauty and hope. I could only be there, holding her wish and intention in my heart and carrying out my duty and honor to support and facilitate ease to the best of my ability.

I actively practiced gratitude for the opportunity to serve in this way. I didn't need to know how and, strangely, it didn't really bother me that I was essentially powerless. I could, though, admire her strength stopping just short of pity for the injustice of how her astonishing fortitude and willpower for being able to make the decision and set all this in motion seemed to be exactly the confirmation of spirit that was getting in the way of her passing on sooner.

Her desire to go was exhausted and she was beyond frustrated that her will could now only be summoned to accept being alive now without much connection with joy. She wanted to be gone, but her body was taking its own time and her spirit was fractured in a fight against pain.

She wasn't afraid, I'm sure of that. Excited if anything in her clearer moments. No room for overthinking it, I was

witnessing a natural gap between biological, intellectu-
al, and soul-level dying on a timing level. Even as it made
sense, I could never have anticipated this before and had
unconsciously assumed, or hoped I guess, that these layers
would all line up in a neat and easy momentary event like
an actor's depiction in the movies or a play.

But nay, real life, real death, is not fair and often mess-
ier. And... if one can be present beyond their own distress,
more beautiful too.

Waiting

"Life is pleasant. Death is peaceful.
It's the transition that's troublesome."
Issac Asimov

Supporting someone in the final weeks of dying is full of things to do and also lots and lots of time spent empty of active purpose, where patience and observing the revolving presence of mind that comes from simply waiting together are all there is to do.

For those less comfortable with silence in the presence of another, the experience could be unnerving but when checking in with the question "Is there anything left to say or do?" continually comes up empty, for me, a precious peacefulness arrives. It's mostly the freedom from having to try to put words on something making way for gentle reverence in being able to share time just sitting and breathing together.

Early in the days of Mary Lou's winding down of life we indulged in light(er), mostly joyful, conversations about how it would all go. In "blissful" ignorance it seemed entirely unnecessary to bring up the down and dirty realities of the more horrible and stress-inducing experiences ahead of us. We envisioned the celebration in the front field surrounded by hills splashed with vibrant colored leaves on a perfect Vermont fall day. We saw a big tent, food, music, and her many friends and family (except for her youngest son) laughing, dancing, and sharing stories and jokes that collectively and poignantly created and affirmed Mary Lou's legacy.

The prospect of this most glorious and fleeting moment of a convening became so compelling that we all wished Mary Lou could be there herself to enjoy. We even flirted with the idea of a "pre-morial," something I'm sure others have orchestrated. But, of course, the event in its purest form was contingent on really only one thing, that she had died.

As time progressed, the projected weekend to plan for continued to push back. The ladies at the Dummerston Grange, who would cater the event, were on standby with periodic communication regarding available dates. The large tent became available following its use at the local school and was even stored at Elysian Hills out of logistical convenience. Outliving all of our anticipations, the prospect of a perfect fall day in Vermont grew from unpredictable, to hopeful, to slim as the days grew shorter and colder. The fleeting brilliance of the fall colors came and went revealing the muted pallor of Vermont's tranquil hills waiting for winter.

Then, somewhere in the last few weeks, the duty of care outpaced any motivation to continue readjusting concrete plans with intent, and the whole thing got put aside. My dad and I vowed that we would do our best, acknowledged that it wouldn't be as flawless as Mary Lou's exacting vision dictated, and affirmed that we would carry the purity of the spirit of the event into whatever happened. We knew that it would be perfect in its own "as good as possible" way. As a longtime hospice volunteer, Dad was well aware of the idea that she could live for weeks or even months more, especially, it seemed, if she continued to rely on the sustenance of popsicles.

Back to the original plan then. "I want to die. I'm going to stop eating and drinking. Let's get on with it." The energy had shifted into a day-by-day monitoring, assessing, reacting, and caring project. Then, hour by hour, with a constant tug and pull of consideration for how our actions collectively were speeding or slowing the process. Leading with the inherently unclear and shifting disposition of Mary Lou's self-expressed discomfort, physically, emotionally, and spiritually, we confronted the full gamut of ways we could try to "help" her out.

"Okay, enough! Give me the big shot of morphine and let's get this over with!" she said one morning. In my own ignorance Mary Lou and I had already discussed an errant understanding that morphine could speed one's dying in an ultimately merciful way. I had observed the use of morphine at the end of others' lives and mistakenly assumed that it was the drug that "caused" the death. Asking the nurses about this to confirm the option, I learned that in actuality, morphine's induction of physical relaxation doesn't cause death as much as allow one to stop fighting long enough to make its more natural occurrence possible. In this way, curiously, the nurse related, it may even prolong death, if only by seconds or minutes, when used at the end.

As I see it now, it has more to do with tempering the horror of a body's active struggle at the time of death than it does anything to do with stopping life. To overdose fatally from morphine would take consuming more on the order of a quart or more of the liquid form. Anything short of that would just result in a long nap from which she would wake, likely in even deeper despair.

Mary Lou wasn't able to swallow that amount of anything even if we were able to acquire that amount, which we couldn't. I had to tell her much to her disappointment as much as to my own internal relief that I had been mistaken earlier and that this wasn't an option after all.

So given that idea was no more than fantasy, what could we do, if she really meant what it sounded like she was saying? It was no longer appropriate or possible, given her wavering state of lucidity, to include her in complex conversations, so Dad and I separately and together considered other forms of "assisted suicide," from Act 39 Vermont's legal pathway for taking one's own life, to more direct and violent end-of-life tactics, we saw choices we were not (yet at least) willing to make.

The process continued and Mary Lou continued to live, not really wanting to at all anymore and wondering in increasing pain and with growing delusion and desperation, when forever and how possibly soon could this happen? There was an element of frustration, even anger, at still being alive some of the time and I could see her will being tested if not broken against the admirable on the one hand and cruel on the other fortitude of her being. Trust and faith were the only ground I could muster to contain enough of my waning strength to continue showing up with compassion and, the wellspring of grace seeming nearly tapped, we dug in.

Days and hours became confused and irrelevant. We would hear her wake probably from a resurgence of pain, following a cycle of medication providing a temporary respite of sleep or at least unconsciousness wearing off, with a familiar refrain of "Good moooorning!" even though it was ten at night. We would follow through with the morning routine of providing a warm washcloth so she could cleanse her face and comb her hair in preparation for the day because these things brought comfort. It didn't matter that her experience was losing touch with reality. Doing these things comforted us too and we honestly didn't know what else to do.

Spelling each other, Dad and I would take breaks from sitting with her. I would go on my walks and runs, staying close enough and conscious to avoid cell phone shadows in case any call to urgency arose. Dad would take short walks to the mailbox or go to the grocery store. I would join scheduled Zoom calls or tend to organizing a presentation I was to do, or further my ongoing fiduciary duties in resolving my mom's estate.

Like waiting in a queue at the bank, or the DMV, an amusement park, or ski area, the eventuality of what we were there to do was on pause and there was nothing to do but hang out and make the best of it. Unlike those situations however, there was increasingly no way to predict or anticipate when Mary Lou's number would come up and remaining alert and at the ready all the time was exhausting.

Singing songs, leading guided meditations, doing healing energy work, adjusting her posture, massaging her feet and legs, sometimes trying to converse, fluffing her pillow, grabbing the corners of the sheet she was on to pull her up on the bed with a coordinated "One, two, three, pull!", changing the water in the flowers someone had brought weeks ago, and just sitting there looking at her are memories burned into me.

One day, I know both Dad and I were hoping our idea that it surely should happen very soon was accurate and as the hospice nurse Jennifer left saying, "I'm not going to put her on my ten-day list yet," I'm not sure how we felt other than dismayed at the prospect of how we could ever navigate two more weeks. Genuine trepidation about what might come with continued degradation and how we would be able to be there hung over us like a still fog.

These nurses became one of our only reliable sources of strength. They were understaffed, driving all over southeastern Vermont every day, providing care for the dying and those around them. Jennifer had more than twenty cases, some like Mary Lou's, others quite different.

Crass as it may sound, in the business hospice nurses wake every day to go to work to do, there actually is a queue of people lined up in front of the door to death. Their professional charge to patiently address each in order based on a combination of readiness and biological actuality is just one of the amazing practicalities juggled in their work every day. When one "earned" ten-day list status, the protocol for care only then escalated to daily visits and so, while having Jennifer's reassurance and the relief we felt in offloading the burden of making decisions while she was there would have been so helpful every day, to ask that of her while she also had others who would actually die tomorrow or this week also needing her was not only impractical, but unreasonable and selfish. An able hospice nurse's ability to witness, catalog, and document a dying person's state of pain and, let's face it, suffering, while bringing unfathomable compassion and gentle bedside presence to all involved was beyond inspirational. This is what they do every day. It was all new to us and we were but capable novices.

I suppose I was grateful for how long it was taking, but I wasn't always happy it was taking so long.

I was feeling a little ashamed or guilty for how weary I was growing, and how much I might be wishing it would happen sooner than later. The agitation of waking each morning or returning from a walk to find Mary Lou still with us was increasingly unavoidable.

We were all growing tired of the schedule for this process being out of our control. But we weren't in control. There was no schedule. Holding the space of being there for some undetermined, unknowable number of days or hours took a lot of energy.

But we knew the time was getting shorter.

Embracing the Unknown

There are moments in life when change happens. A precious experience when an event we have been anticipating as an entirely new context for life arrives and an air of heightened awareness surrounds us.

Like the birth of my child, my first day in the third grade, or beginning a new job in a foreign country, the honor of being able to share in Mary Lou's dying stopped everything else in my life. It shed a light of perspective that made what was rote and routine about my daily to-do's easy to let go of. There was no need to push or fight for accomplishment or progress in the domains of work, other family matters, or training for my next long run. It was clear that in the grand scheme of things, this carried status as a rite of passage and all that was important was to bear witness to change, surrender to the unknown, and be present for what would come next.

As I reflect on these moments of transformation experienced, I find a longing to be able to live a life where every moment could occur with such ease and grace. Yet, it seems inevitably human somehow that what follows is a return to a more mundane baseline. The excitement of new possibilities so present at the apex of a moment that felt like it changed me forever would fade as familiarity returned. Over and over, I would, often with some disappointment, realize that while the context of life was new and different, I somehow didn't feel changed.

I honestly hope I never settle or resign myself to life as I know it going on without real change. But the experience of finding that while everything has changed nothing is different is one of life's bittersweet gifts.

Dad and I knew that Mary Lou would be here with us one minute and soon, we would still be here, and she would be gone. The fatigue of tending to ourselves and each other along the way both allowed for this air of raw truth to settle on to us veiling any urgency in other matters, and also buffered, in a way, our capacity to take it all in at the moment.

Practical matters of preparing and eating meals, making arrangements with the newspaper for her obituary, the funeral home for her cremation, and the town Grange for her celebration event became our solace. With as much heart as we could muster, we shared with family, friends, and neighbors eager to learn how things were going. We listened as these people showed up, often yearning, even nearly begging, to offer support, all the while knowing that was truthfully impossible, and, with a combination of compassion, pain, and acquiescence, not necessary either. Maintaining consistency and familiarity in tending to basic daily needs became a sort of meditation as we anticipated a totality of change or transformation we couldn't fathom.

Chop wood. Carry water.

Unlike the miracle of birth, the wonder of death presents a different kind of opening. An anticipation of something undefinable, laden with all sorts of meaning to be made, unavoidable and uncontrollable. A basic natural fact of nature bearing nothing but the simplicity of reverence. The wonder and hope of a newly birthed life, yet to be shaped and realized, decidedly carries more spontaneous joy than the mysteries surrounding death. But when embracing change, however it feels, that affect of experiencing is more a facade in the presence of an utter not knowing of what will really happen next. Then, as always, the nervous excitement of facing something unknown transforms as I find what's really there after all is still me. Just now with a fresh perspective with which to continue seeking understanding.

Lying in my bed as Mary Lou was living through her dying in the other room, as I thought about it, the passing of my life as I knew it before when my child's fresh little body entered the world with all the hope and promise of a future yet to unfold was not that different from the arrival of a new possibility in my life as Mary Lou's body stopped renewing itself and returned to the earth.

With other deaths in other circumstances in my past, I'd settled for treating the experience of a loved one dying as a change I didn't plan for, want, or invite. Perhaps true but when used as an excuse, I could see that these abdications led to snags of guilt, pain, blame, and shame when weathering the ensuing grief. So, I could see that to stop there leaves me powerless in the face of the possibility of discovering the ways my new life is now different.

As the three of us sat together during what turned out to be Mary Lou's final day, I considered the different relationship each of us had with this change. For Mary Lou, I couldn't know for sure, but projected that on some level, she was finding (hopefully) peace in letting go of her body. She was so near the freedom of being done. Watching Dad, I couldn't fathom the depth of his experience as he would yet have to surrender to a new life without his partner's physical company and presence. It felt daunting that for him the hardest part was just beginning. For me? I had to step over a sense of being too selfish in considering how this change was also mine to embrace to see that my version of what lay waiting in the looming unknown would only reveal itself to the extent that I was able to let go and allow something in me to die too.

As grueling as the last month had been, here we were with the peace of nothing left to say and very little left to do for now. Whatever would come next no longer had to be planned, controlled, or directed in any way. I felt a calm subdued joy in knowing I didn't have to rush to understanding of what my future would reveal. I was in awe of Mary Lou's capacity to have anticipated this somehow when she decided to go in the way she did. Her generosity in offering this gift, not knowing how or even if it would be received fully, revealed a profound foundation of her legacy for me.

Whatever would come next was mine to discover and if I could bring as much strength and determination to get out of my own way as she had, whatever lay ahead would surely be even more full of life for me and everyone I touch.

The waiting was over and whenever she died, it would be okay.

It took time but after more reflection I've learned that when I'm more of an active participant in my own experience of major changes, the awkwardness of embracing something unfamiliar yields a more conscious and healthy feeling. A cleansing shedding of the old and growing to understand and accept something new. Seeing Mary Lou die so honestly and without reservation made this clearer for me.

Change happens all the time but to be transformed on any level is a possibility held by every moment whenever I choose to accept it.

Doors and Windows

———

Any doorway invokes transition.
Windows invite a dance of imagination.

As Mary Lou approached the threshold of her passing, I could only suppose of her experience, but the gift of a chance to peer through windows of insight and reflection instilled something for me to dance with. How might my own mortality unfold in my remaining hours, days, years, or decades?

What one sees through a window is theirs alone, and each personal filter of intentions, experience, predilections, and fears is sometimes more of what is worth noticing than whatever might actually be there. Perhaps the idea that the view of our final destination is commonly and most easily related as moving toward a light is evidentiary of our capacity to accept this fact. In masking any recognizable or describable qualities of a view of what lies ahead and freely giving up any arrogance in naming what's so for another, we invoke together the mystery of blindness. But with more trust than fear for the difference of occlusion resulting from the brilliance of a divine light rather than the consuming depletion of utter darkness. Qualities of giving rather than taking. A big bang of birth emanating rather than a crushing collapse of black hole-level disappearance.

The idea of being surrounded by loved ones at the moment of death might be born of fear, vanity, love, or any such construct of desire to share in a relationship to the very end. The situations I've experienced where small cadres of family, friends, and caregivers have gathered to witness, support, and share in the dying of another have mostly borne a result where the one dying has still seemed to choose to go privately and alone. Perhaps embarrassed by the naked intimacy of the act? Out of compassion for the possible pain experienced by others? Selfish in hoarding the experience alone? Desperately alone and disappointed at the last in a mistake of uncaring or lapse of attention from others? Ultimately content, complete, and at peace? Who knows?

Perhaps the causes of happenstance, if there are any, relate more to the capacity of those present to be with the reality of a person actually dying. Anyone too uncomfortable to be in such a position wouldn't show up. Others might be present out of respect or curiosity but might be subconsciously guided to find convenience in avoiding the moment by having gone to the bathroom, stepped out for a break from the intensity, found themselves called away by a phone call, or other tasks of greater-feeling priority. In any case, no matter what transpires in planning and holding space for something anticipated . . . it happens when and how it happens. And then, the stories continue to be written and told as the fact recedes into the realms of past experience.

We are not human beings having a spiritual experience, but are spiritual beings having a human experience.
Pierre Telliard De Chardin

What Do I Have to Lose?

———

E mpathy can be confusing for me. I frequently lose track of what's mine and what's not when serving another person. Often, giving up some version of the idea that it's all about me lends a more grounded perspective on what I can give up in seeking more of what I need.

In witnessing Mary Lou's passing, as a participant in the process and also observer, the presence of loss was a shared experience. She was doing the dying, not me, or so it seemed. This hesitation revealed another betrayal of how the oneness of truth trumps my egoic sense of self-importance, how spirit and soul live independent of physical existence. We were both dying and, when at our best, both choosing to live gracefully and joyfully as the dying happened.

Anything I had projected about the apparently poignant blend of pain, purpose, and bliss she was feeling as her life continued to end was also mine to embody. I could

feel a palpable sense of freedom in the anticipatory slip-
stream of relief that it was now almost over.

I had with intention, or at least acceptance, lost myself
along the way and now began the process of finding myself
anew. Of course, this opportunity is present in every moment, yet also reveals itself as a process while the change
itself unfolds across the arc of one's life.

Sitting with her, I wondered how much waiting to die
is no different from waiting to live. At least I knew with
each next breath that I wasn't done yet.

As I've shared, putting others ahead of myself has
been one of the biggest themes of my dharma. I've suf-
fered for it greatly. I've also engineered amazing success
in plying the nearly unavoidable habit and being lauded for my generosity, intuitive depth, and selflessness. I
even made a career of it as a service professional. Anyone
drawn to work in healing or hospitality is deft in anticipating the needs of others and satisfying them before they
even occur to those we're serving as something missing.
The best of us can do this without sacrificing ourselves
along the way, but it took me many years to come to that. I
worked in this capacity long enough to suffer the drain of
putting my needs last, not even seeing them anymore and
never really getting to them.

Having walked this path for most of my life I approached the call to support Dad and Mary Lou with the
benefit of self-awareness. Yet, as choosing to serve on the

edges of my own capacity and beyond always is, I was barely capable of conceding my own limitations and maintaining healthy boundaries.

Being in the presence of her honest suffering, I saw how I could more easily retreat to my "safe place" of sacrifice and suffering in giving more of myself than necessary to try and alleviate her plight. I could also see how the best thing I could do for her was to not lose track of doing the best for me. This took effort, but I ended up less confused about whose suffering was whose and in choosing to accept mine and do something about it, being with hers felt less painful for both of us.

Choosing to let go of self-sacrifice has only been the beginning of another leg of my journey for which living in the unknown of all knowing is only the trailhead. My friend's philosophical foundation shared with me long ago comes to mind again: "All I know is that I know that I don't know, and that is all I know." Socrates arrived at that place many years ago, and I think we would all do well to get there for ourselves.

So far, the work of receiving with the same generosity that I give has included discipline in practicing the letting go of long-held past ideas so as to be more loving and nakedly generous without selling out to facetious humor, backhanded judgment, or the act of running away.

Now reduced to doable choices when relating to others, the feeling of how simple the task is yet how strong the currents of habit and fabricated social pressure seem is likely a sign that I'm forging the river in the right place for now. I know that my fear of being undercut and swept away and losing everything I once held as purposeful is nothing to excuse me from moving forward anyway. My survival, my life, could never be behind me but for what lies ahead. If the river of transformation has its way with my attempts to grasp at balance, eliminating the crutch of a sense of sure footing, so be it.

I realized I could make plans to die in a certain way too. But witnessing so much death lately and now sharing Mary Lou's version of approaching her life's end freed me to live without knowing or needing to predetermine how it will come to pass. I was watching her surrender the illusion of control while playing it out anyway, as if it were possible to direct the process and yet knowing that it would happen on its own when and however it did anyway.

This new level of acceptance of the inevitability of death now provides me the opportunity to embrace the inevitability of living while the myriad reactions, responses, and calculations involved in humanizing my experience become obligatory in all their meaninglessness.

Natural Causes

———

I believe these words appeared on Mary Lou's death certificate as Lila officially declared and documented the occurrence. Given all that had transpired, even the idea that anyone could decide how it had happened and name it seemed oddly arrogant and incomplete.

What about a certificate of life? What would be on that form?

I can't remember if Mary Lou and I ever discussed the idea of dying "naturally" in so many words. She did, though, make it clear that she didn't want to be kept alive through artificial means, leaving the implication at least that nature's course was primary for her. When it was time for her body to die, then let it be so.

As I see it, to settle for the descriptor "natural causes" is to skip over so much of the remarkable power and grace she employed at the end. Biologically, the miracle of death is as profound as the miracles of conception and birth. Not possible without human involvement yet undeniably out of our hands in the moment and challenging to explain without acknowledging some higher power or unified energy. For me, the word *natural* satisfies this spiritual quality just fine but what of the unique nature of the human part? Wouldn't it be better, since we mostly still live in a paradigm that is more comfortable separating human and natural, to call it what it is? Died of humanness? Died of living? Died of death?

As far as cause goes, Mary Lou's dying was clearly made possible by human intervention. Starting with her own, actively depriving her own body's natural living process by exerting her will and ceasing to give it the necessary nutrients for continued life. And further, through all the actions the nurses, Dad, I, and others undertook in support of her wish. These all can be seen in support of nature's course I guess, but why not embrace the fact that in our humanness as nature, or relationship to nature if you must, we exercised agency and the capacity to control or influence Mary Lou's living biological system? As a species, we have harnessed enough understanding of chemistry to have most of our socially allowed (if not accepted) forms of causing death involve the intervention of drugs, from those used in palliative care to the pharmaceutical cocktails involved in assisted suicide or capital punishment. While these artificially engineered molecules don't always succeed in fulfilling our intentions, for me it seems like they do stack the deck of causation against any higher power's design for an individual's continued existence if such a thing exists.

Most of us have grown up in a paradigm that filters our experience through an idea that humans and nature are somehow separate yet connected. As a false duality, which is inclusive or dominant of the other could be argued either way. On this level, invoking the idea that a death occurred "naturally" might be the only attempt at providing a link to being at peace with what happened on a more spiritual level. Farcical really, for it doesn't take much to agree that all deaths occur naturally.

Avoiding the pitfall of the inherent incapacity for language to accurately describe anything, I wonder what might appear on a certificate of death, if one were even necessary, in a/the "new" paradigm? As we evolve and awaken to new language with the capacity to better relate from oneness, would there be more honesty offered by the words "died of human causes"? Would stating the idea that there was a cause at all even be necessary in all cases?

What participating with Mary Lou's dying allowed me to see was a desire for more social acceptance around both the life and death giving capacity we wield as humans. Again, not a theological question or one to be addressed by the muddled musings of applied quantum physics for me, but more a living paradigm-level choice to be frank about the nature of our nature.

In being with Mary Lou as she was dying, I noticed that the only thing I might be afraid of in death anymore is not participating in its expression of life. I can ponder how I might want to die all I want, but the only use in this is the way these thoughts clear the fog of my not entirely conscious approach to living now. Shifting the question from "How do I want to die?" to "How am I dying?" enables keener perception of actions I can take in living wholly, including doing so as an expression of dying.

I'm not talking about survival here, for that is honestly separate from living or dying. In fact, I think that a drive to simply survive is probably not much more than an act of resignation to life at best through some idea that maybe someday, "if I live long enough," I'll find a purity of self-expression or a peace in full-purpose living that is a worthy enough place from which to die. Some sort of agreement to press the "pause" button on any mandate to live fully along with a hope or plan to resume active living should whatever threat to survival resolve to find us still alive.

Here we were. Mary Lou was simultaneously at the mercy of "nature's" natural course and suffering the result of her ultimately human choice in action. She didn't seem to be wondering if describing it a certain way mattered, I thought, so why should I?

The Sound of Silence

———

"Silence is more musical than any song."
Christina Rossetti

Straining to hear any sound of her breathing, which had grown shallow and faint, I held my own breath listening to the quiet. Was this it? Had it happened? I held back hope for a minute that this more than month-long process might be over and had to make sure.

Dad and I had been sitting in silence with Mary Lou in the living room which, I realize now, having been rearranged to accommodate her hospital bed and other best attempts at service and comfort, had been transformed into the "dying" room temporarily. He, in a chair by her side holding her hand, and me, a few feet away in a recliner chair.

Comforted to be together yet trying to keep a measure of distance out of respect for the intimacy of their privacy, I half averted my attention with a newspaper crossword puzzle I had been mostly stumped by for a few days. This also served to keep me awake as it was after 8 p.m., and being a morning person, I could have easily been dozing.

Dad stood up and left the room, saying he was going outside for a walk to get some fresh air and stretch his legs.

It was then I noticed, along with the whirring hum of the pump continually shifting the air in the mattress to help avoid bed sores and the ticking of the wall clock . . . I could hear stillness. Like the silent sound of new fallen snow, there was a timeless pause hanging in the air that wasn't there before.

I got up and went to her side, so aware that it was just me there for now. Not wanting to call out to Dad before confirming the state of things, I picked up her hand and leaned over to ask if she was there with me. The lack of a conscious response wasn't enough evidence, as she had spent most of the last dozen hours or so deep in stillness. I knew that to gaze upon a dead body often plays tricks on our senses, thinking we see signs of breathing and hints of movement that aren't real. I wouldn't have been surprised if her body jerked in a half-waking response to the pain that had become the dominant feature of her last days in her body. I recognized my denial and hung on to it, because I had been fooled by my hope for this moment so many times in the past week. Somewhat conflicted, I lifted her right leg, which had been the biggest unavoidable center of her discomfort and, apologizing to her out loud I said, "I'm sorry, Mary Lou, but I have to be sure," as I shook it gently at first, then with more vigor.

Nothing.

Like the loudness of the silence that echoes as it emerges following an orchestra's last note and just before the roar of applause, a reverence for all that had transpired before arrived with a sigh of relief. With my attention immediately shifting to Dad, I took a minute to stroke her hair, place a kiss on her forehead, and tell her "Good job, Mary Lou. You did it! I'm going to go get Dad now."

I found him in the drive just outside the front door. It was dark and as we approached each other I said, "She's gone."

"She's gone?" he repeated, his voice breaking a little, confirming that even with his challenged hearing he had understood.

"Yes," I replied, and in silence he returned to her side.

Marking the Moment

———

After a short minute, we might have exchanged some words, I can't remember, but we agreed that it was early enough, barely, to invoke the plan we had made for what would happen at this point. I got up and went to the dining room, confirming that I would call on the five people Dad had arranged to come for a simple ritual to prepare her body and acknowledge her death.

This part of the plan was of his creation. A couple of weeks earlier he had asked Mary Lou if she was okay with having the closest women in her life come to wash and dress her body followed by a shared meditation of sorts where her daughter would anoint her with essential oils as he led a reading invoking all the parts of her body. Her reply, another sign of her clarity and readiness, as well as a sweet display of their loving partnership was simply to say, "That's up to you. I'll be gone so do whatever feels right for you."

And so, after spreading the news, everyone confirmed they would make their way to the farm. Even though, past everyone's bedtime and some with forty-five-minute drives, they would be there. It was near midnight when the lead hospice nurse signed the official notice of death and we proceeded. Mary Lou's daughter, daughter-in-law, massage therapist, and another dear friend cleaned and dressed her in a cheery red outfit in line with her insistence on banning anything black or invoking of sadness in her wake. They did this in private, for her "Victorian upbringing" as she called it would never have been comfortable with men seeing her nakedness in any way. Then, we all gathered in chairs near her, taking turns reading pieces she and Dad had come to find meaning in and sharing feelings and stories affirming her strength and the joy of living with her.

Some would call it bittersweet, and not be wrong, the poignance and glory of stillness when in the presence of a body still cooling from its living state. This was one case where an unavoidable sense of relief was welcome but still shared only in the unspoken. The goal had been reached but the journey wasn't by any means over. We had only reached the top of the mountain and faced little time for celebration now as the new goal of returning back down would be best approached with as much care and attention as the climb. Life's gravity was still an ever-present force but navigating in harmony with its natural pressure rather than moving against its grain would be a new and welcome experience.

By 1:30 a.m. or so, everyone parted with hugs and smiles. Even though it would have been fine, no tears were shed, which was one of the things Mary Lou insisted was not required in the spirit of celebration she wanted us all to be present to. Dad settled into his chair next to her, where he had been sleeping since I had arrived and I retired to bed, falling into sleep quickly and with a sense of peace that I didn't need to be alert enough to arise should she need anything urgently overnight.

For now, though, we could all rest. There would be time to return the room to its primary purpose as a living space and take stock of what newness awaited in the perpetuation of life at Elysian Hills.

Like noticing negative space (in artistic terms) defining a piece of art that makes it come alive, we would come to stand back and view her life, in all its raw glory and truth, admiring the emptiness as blank canvas now expanding with new boundaries of its frame fading to nothing.

Pancakes

"Griddle cakes, pancakes, hot cakes, flapjacks: why are there four names for grilled batter and only one word for love?"

George Carlin

The morning after Mary Lou passed was a Sunday, which traditionally saw Dad making pancakes, "panacakes" as he's always called them, for breakfast. Her body was waiting in the living room where the events following her passing at around 8:30 p.m. the evening before left her clean, dressed in her best red outfit, and gently blessed by close family and friends as part of the ritual Dad had orchestrated.

I met Dad in the kitchen around 8 a.m. and said, "Good morning!" in the way that Mary Lou always said it, hollering from the other room so as to be heard and noticed: "Good moooooooorning!" and asked if he wanted pancakes.

"No," he said "I don't feel like it."

After a moment I replied, "Well I want pancakes. Would you like to join me and have some?"

"Yes! That would be great," he said, and we both smiled.

And with that we were off together on the fresh start of finding ground again and now without Mary Lou, at least in body.

We had plenty to keep us busy, which was good, and although we were both exhausted on so many levels from the preceding weeks' intensity, the relief from the constant need to be attentive and alert to Mary Lou's moment-by-moment comfort and care was welcome, if not a bit strange.

We could now go on walks together rather than spelling each other in our shared duty to be close by. Even out to restaurants and other excursions. That evening or the next, while driving down the hill for dinner, Dad commented that it felt odd, like he was playing hooky.

It was precious to be with Dad at this time, and this was what Mary Lou had wanted.

Dust to Dust

———

Finishing our pancakes there was much to do now that the ordeal of Mary Lou's dying no longer commanded all of our attention and energy. Absurd-feeling practicalities we had prepared for were now up to be carried out. The lingering cocoon of intimacy and reverence still afforded us strength in acting from shared purpose as we continued caring gently for all that Mary Lou was in the world with a sense of duty and honor.

Her body was still in the family room, lying now oddly flat, relaxed, and unburdened of any pain in being alive. Like being unable not to look while passing an accident on the highway, gazing upon her dead body dressed in red, mouth agape, was equally seductive in its grotesqueness and as a vision of beauty in having arrived at its long-anticipated state of final rest and peace.

Not quite final rest I guess though, as there was a knock at the door, and we went to greet two men from the mortuary who had arrived to transport her body for cremation. I was in full support mode, and thankfully so, as I couldn't imagine what my dad might be feeling, and grateful that I could at least spare him any unnecessary distraction in having to make simple decisions regarding the logistics of getting her body out of the house. Having moved my mom's dead body less than a year earlier, "this wasn't my first rodeo," as Mary Lou might have said if she were watching.

So in a flash of eye contact with the mortuary workers I resolved their concerns on how best to achieve their goal of getting her body to the SUV hearse with sensitivity for Dad and efficiency at the same time. I knew that while in full rigor mortis, lifting, tilting, and moving the body down the narrow hallway around corners and out the front door would be easy work for the three of us. I also anticipated how it would feel oddly heavy in spite of her frail and withered state, like a wooden beam not yet dry. The three of us also knew, without having to say so out loud, that getting this part done with right care and haste would be the most compassionate thing we could offer Dad in having to watch as his beloved wife left Elysian Hills on the start of her body's next and final journey.

A few days later, Dad exclaimed, "I'm heading out to go get Mary Lou!" Returning after picking up her ashes and running another errand or two, we reveled in her return to the farm albeit in a very different form. Having not been physically away from Elysian Hills for more than a few hours at a time in probably a decade or more, surely she would have been excited and beaming to be home.

We discovered a suitable small wooden box with simple dovetailed joinery among the last of her "stuff" we'd collected, still waiting in the mud room to find a new home. Placing the plastic bag of ash that was Mary Lou inside, the box found its place on the dining table where she could return, for now, to sharing her presence at our daily meals at 8:00 a.m., noon, and 5 p.m. Her presence, even without voice, made for a welcome and healing sense of companionship in our conversations at the table while we all awaited her interment ceremony planned for the evening following the celebration coming up in a couple more weeks.

The Celebration

———

When a Vermonter is asked if they've lived there their
whole life, they reply,
"Not yet."

I f you don't know someone steeped in, or at least related to, the unique qualities of Vermont, consider the cul-
tural influences of the region. As the only landlocked state
in New England, Vermont has always held the promise of
acceptance for self-made people. A haven for seekers from
indigenous natives to French Canadian immigrants, early
English colonists, settlers from the waves of immigration
from Europe and other continents, and lots of hippies; if
you lived near the northeast corner of America and wanted
to get back to the land, live a simple and good life, exercise
your independent spirit, and do your own thing, Vermont
was waiting for you.

So, picture a sanctuary for free thinkers and hard
workers and you'll begin to understand the grounded

honesty and concise, if not terse, economy of words true Vermonters bring to relating and expressing themselves.

To call out "true" Vermonters may sound prideful or even arrogant, and it probably is, but only in the best ways. Despite their collective century plus years living in the state, neither Mary Lou nor Dad could claim the appellation of *Vermonter*. I was born and grew up there but also never considered myself a Vermonter as my parents and grandparents weren't born there. Yet, I never once was made to feel like an outsider. I always admired the way growing up in a culture actively holding generations of wisdom with unabashed pride and confidence made me feel.

I share all this here foundationally to the flavors of love, truth, and blunt honesty that rang through Mary Lou and Dad's small town of Dummerston, home to about 1,800 people, as news of her passing spread.

Now, already early November, the air was crisp, and people were buttoning up their farms and homes for winter. Planning for an outdoor event was beyond practical anymore and we had set up the main room of the East Dummerston Grange Hall as the gathering place for Mary Lou's community to join in celebration of her life. Despite the lingering fear of the risk of COVID among a decidedly elderly group, more than eighty people arrived to pay their respects.

As the event commenced, serving as the emcee, not officiant or minister which were both within my capacity but not at all what she wanted, I did my best to "channel"

Mary Lou's intentions for a unique and lively "memorial," setting the tone with some of the prescribed music and readings, and opening the floor for anyone to give voice to remembrances and declarations of their experiences with Mary Lou.

What followed was almost two hours of sharing, some planned ahead along with many spontaneous orations from more than half of those present. Even some of the most introverted and microphone-shy people felt safe standing to address the room.

The natural eloquence of humility from those embracing the courage to speak enveloped the room invoking more shared laughter than tears, just as Mary Lou had hoped and planned. I took a measure of pride in sharing personal stories of things that no one else probably knew about her and am certain that the tapestry of words we all shared offered everyone the chance to elevate their connection and cultivate a more nuanced education of who she was.

A full range of wisdom shared via everything from sincere quotes and sayings, worthy of being hung on a wall in a country home, to irreverence and humor found its way out into the open. Her "playlist" of musical numbers was sprinkled throughout, keeping the mood and energy on track with her vision with everything from "Somewhere Over The Rainbow" to Dad and Mary Lou's cherished "Wherever You Go" sung by the local Weston Priory Monks, to rousing renditions of "Turkey In The Straw," "Happy Trails," and Mary Lou's pièce de résistance closing number, "Off We Go into the Wild Blue Yonder."

There was even a collection of more items to be given away on tables near the door, for which I did my best Mary Lou sales pitch encouraging attendees to take whatever they wanted in support of Mary Lou's intention to not see anything disposed of that may have continued meaning for someone else.

Ideas about Mary Lou I had hung on to with some measure of judgment that served to limit my sharing of love vanished and an entirely new perspective on who she was and why she did the things she did came into view. So much of her "lifeness" was still present, only now in the possibility of ongoing transformation through embracing new and unforeseen reflections in our relationship.

Following the public event we returned to Elysian Hills, less than three miles away, for a more private informal interment ceremony at the family cemetery. The small group of six of us present were sufficiently sated from all that had been exchanged at the Grange and followed through with the duty of seeing Mary Lou's ashes properly committed to the lasting embrace of her beloved Elysian Hills.

As we dispersed, strolling each at our own pace back along the 100 yards or so of dirt road to the house, a blanket of satisfied completion settled on each of us holding all the stillness emerging as we all came down from a day packed with a lifetime of poignant anticipation, excitement, joy, and reverence. Dad and I shared a quiet evening with the peacefulness born of being both energized and exhausted.

The next day was a bit of an encore with a spacious yet determined schedule. After Dad and I shared breakfast with my cousin, his sister's daughter, who had traveled from Virginia to attend, I went to retrieve the last items from the Grange, while they continued their visit. Then, following a Zoom-based offering of the celebration event for those unable or unwilling to attend the in-person version and a shared walk to the cemetery, I left. Knowing there would be no good time to have Dad find himself alone at home, and also eager to return to my wife, two dogs, and life in Wyoming, Dad and I shared an embrace, took a joyous selfie, and away I went watching in the rear-view mirror as Dad waved me off.

Driving away, all I was present to was how each day alive is, in its simplest terms, filled with all the things we choose to do now sandwiched between an acknowledgment of completions and witnessing the emergence of new opportunities. I made a vow to myself that I had made a number of times before. I promised that I would keep this freeing clarity of perspective and simple purity of experience awake and consciously part of every day from now on.

In the End, It's Just Death

—

The death of a loved one doesn't always occur as a big deal. Sometimes, we don't have the perspective, time, or desire to really be with it all at once when it happens. I don't think we always get to choose how deeply or when the experience touches us though.

Illusions of control aside, whenever someone we had a relationship with dies, no matter how long we knew them, how much or how little we shared, how authentic or intimate, guarded, emotional, or purely pragmatic the exchanges were, something about the possibility of future involvement with them now having changed seems worth at least considering.

The opportunity to relate anew that was always there doesn't go away. Generating and expressing things like gratitude, forgiveness, compassion, and love don't require two-way communication to hold meaning and value. The chance to own what's ours, reflect on the gift of another's attention (kind or not), and discover something new about ourselves that changes who we are in the moment is always there.

These insights and revelations don't have to be momentous; in fact I find so often that they aren't. That we can't help but be changed by them and can't go back to life before we had a particular realization brings something new to what we can now go on to offer others. Our capacity to "be" in the world shifts, and for me at least, that is something to honor and embrace.

Sometimes, the change is relief in letting go of something we expended energy maintaining in a relationship. Sometimes it reveals the dissolution of a wall, an artifact of identity, or the feeling that there were things we couldn't discuss or share for fear of judgment or harm. Sometimes, the change is bittersweet, like noticing that we missed an opportunity to have them hear us say "I love you" one more time, or perhaps ever. Sometimes, it opens a door to elation in being free to carry the best of what another person was for you forward, to honor them and memorialize their glory by embodying your own version of it and enjoy sharing the same or similar gift with others still living.

No matter what, death is a fact of nature and whatever we do or don't do with it is up to us. Sharing what we experience though can bear fruit for life, even as it takes time to ripen.

Gone in a Flash

—

Shooting stars streak by
All our wishes coming true
Darkness leaks with joy
Haiku by Paul Schmidt

This morning, now almost a full year after she passed, I saw five shooting stars on my daily wake-up meditation walk in the early morning darkness and thought of Mary Lou's life. I played with the metaphor, supposing her existence as a similar flash of distinction. Like a shooting star, something that if I was gifted the fortune of bearing witness to was unavoidably and with an air of seductiveness beautiful. Then gone in a flash.

I love it when I see a shooting star. Perhaps because of the fleeting brilliance that catches my eye and heart without any possibility of not stopping to notice. Also, I can't seem to feel anything other than a sense of awe and wonder, a brief feeling of excitement and happiness that, when it fades, leaves only peace in its wake.

Wishing upon a star, making a wish when seeing a shooting star, or blowing out candles on a birthday cake are all time-honored mini rituals shared as an invitation to focus one's attention inward, granting internal voice and power to the sanctity of prayer. Engaging in these practices is ultimately a private experience set up to be one of momentary connection with the universe of oneness. In its purest form these private wishes are meant to be held secret in the specificity of their formation as words or feelings held in our conscious minds. A breathless pause of worship if you will, with a sense of freedom from the challenge of trying to share. A respectful allowance of shared reverence without words. This license, even mandate, to make a wish—*any* wish—allows a moment of trusting together that there is love everywhere even though we could never possibly describe it fully.

Like never being able to view the entire skyscape of stars at once, we attribute the witnessing of a shooting star to some occurrence of fortune for which the viewer alone has been blessed. And for which a sense of undeniable sacredness invites a chance to pause in reverence and playfully steal a chance to feel ourselves expand to the size of the universe for a few seconds.

On a grand scale, none of our lives are any more meaningful or significant than a hunk of rock flying through the universe, perhaps older than our solar system, hurtling to extinction in a burst of fire traversing its path, only visible to our earthbound eyes from its ignition to the disappearance of the light emitted as it dies.

So brief and yet so distinct, this idea of how my life might emulate that is compelling and comforting somehow.

Witnessing a death has the same air of unrelatable connection to the oneness of all things. A sanctity of peaceful truth in the presence of which I can only become silent, filled with a shower of every emotion at once mashed together with no need to force understanding. I'm nothing but grateful for this experience, even if the complications of my living relationship with the now dead person sometimes cloud my ability to settle for its grace.

All that comes before, all the words and stories and experiences and meaning-making, are folly. Along with everything made up after the fact in our attempts to hang on to the life now over. Attempting to describe our experience of knowing the person, never able to fully relate its unique brilliance without simply being silent in trust and knowing that it happened. Perhaps also hoping that surely others who had the chance to share in life with them as well noticed something miraculous too?

Something akin to the green flash offered by the setting sun to those with the patience and presence to see it, the extended moments of a dying person's actual passing offer a flash of beauty preceded by the brilliance of a life being lived and followed by a dimming to equally brilliant dark.

I could tell stories of my relationship with Mary Lou as I remember it now, but never without the new truth offered by my capacity to make sense of it after the fact of her death. Tapping a wellspring of endless opportunity, I can choose to invoke her life in my memory, as a reflection for mine any time I wish. I can look for gifts and, if I have the courage, draw myself closer to the mirror of reflection our relationship offered. Since she is no longer here, I find it easier to approach more closely than I felt comfortable in her living presence.

The closer one gets to a mirror, the wider its reflection becomes like the phenomenon which captures a larger scope of image the smaller the aperture in a pinhole camera. Even though I had a relatively distant relationship with Mary Lou, her death somehow gives me license to share my own version of intimacy without risking the judgment of social impropriety. I'm free to have my own experience and learn from her deepest offering of love as I see it, for the boundaries of separation between what's hers and what's mine have dissolved. As such, I hope you go beyond your own experience of reading this as having anything to do with Mary Lou, unless you too can accept that she is you.

Finding truth is just the start as long as I realize that I have yet to die. Sharing it becomes the stuff of living fully.

Summoning the courage to continue choosing to live as an expression of my highest truth is the only work I could do for now that really matters.

I can only hope that others might bear witness to the flash of light my life only could be. And if they don't, that they have the supreme chance to witness anyone's life, clear and whole, from start to finish, in just a flash of joyful sharing for as long as they are here with us and with as little time as they may have left.

Dead but Not Gone

———

I think I'm more prone to indulging in feelings of shame, regret, and guilt than my dad. The grace in his example for me in accepting things as they are along with the time I had with both him and Mary Lou during this "event" left me with little to nothing to mull over in this area. The lack of these feelings with Mary Lou, in contrast to some of the other losses I'm grieving and integrating now, has shown me how to be gentler with myself in all cases.

So, I bring this up here more because this platform gives me a chance to shed another layer of this habit of beating myself up over fixed ideas of having "should have" said more, come clean about something, or summoned the courage to make amends for hurt I may have caused someone before they died.

It's nice on one level to think that in death all is forgiven automatically but, at least for me, to embody that takes a bit of work. This topic is more part of the grieving process than the dying process perhaps. I'll probably explore this fully in a future book, but I feel it bears a mention here in case any feelings of incompleteness or unease are getting in the way of being at peace with the fact of someone having died.

The good news with all this, I feel, is that the opportunities to heal toward a space of forgiveness and allowing deeper love to surface, perhaps for the first time even, in a relationship don't go away when the other person dies. In some ways, they become easier to embrace if I choose to do the work of accepting and loving myself more.

To feel shame or regret seems a selfish indulgence in the near wake of coming to know someone has died. Whether we were there at the moment, find out much later, or even have to fully give up the possibility of sharing together while both are still living, this is the stuff of murk in a relationship. A fog or film of reality that grows as a fetid source of undesirable evidence of decay. Totally natural and not to be disallowed or run from as much as accepted to the extent we can tolerate its presence and let go of our urge to repulse. We can fool ourselves into thinking these feelings get buried along with their body but inasmuch as they are ours alone, the costs of this self-subversion can be ironically deadly.

Being with the haunting honesty of regrets is one of the cornerstones of learning from our past relationships carried forth. With some, like family, or perhaps anyone who has touched us deeply enough to have shaped the development of our everyday sense of self, these thoughts arise and linger like echoes repeating as new opportunities to let go. I'm not great at accepting myself when these feelings arrive. I know from experience, at least on a cognitive level, that their presence heralds an opportunity to generate self-acceptance and love. But I tend to hesitate for my unwillingness to let go of whatever I stepped over when the seed of their creation was sowed in refusing to share my love fully in the past.

Similarly, in the space of choosing how to react when a loved one dies is confusing the actual and matter-of-fact loss with an idea that we've also been robbed of the chance to continue enjoying the love and light we knew together before they passed. I see this as part of the confusion confronted in grieving where we are challenged to rewire the substance of a relationship so what is now gone can go without sacrificing all that still continues. I've stumbled through these twists and turns of dysfunction and self-identity in grief enough to see how healing forward through transformation is a measure easier when done with help, guidance, and intention.

All manner of techniques and systems for growing more whole through the careful rewriting of past constructs and calming the ripples of trauma that may have ensued are available in many forms of therapy and healing work. In the end, though, nothing can solve or resolve the harsh edges of these reverberations for us. The compassion or skill of a genuine facilitated healing experience only brings us to a threshold from which, if we're perceptive enough, we can see the possibility, even understand the whys and hows of a separation created and maintained. From there, we can gain a measure of relief and feel energized in this insight. But to confuse having that insight with the actual embodied unraveling of the grip of remaining committed to the design of our story of momentary demise as a "child of God" leaves us destined to repeat the lesson.

What I'm saying is that maybe transformation doesn't happen *to* us as much as it might seem. Somewhere, in each resurrection and wholesale rebuilding of our selves renewed, we allow ourselves to let go of something we decided and then held onto, usually for fear of losing our life. The natural necessity of such fabrications of meaning and our decided responses leave no room for judgment as our ego's survival is mostly hardwired alongside our physical existence.

To be able to let go with some intention is a skill that need not be learned, acquired, or aspired to. It is innate and already present, becoming an ally when nurtured and cultivated through the sureness of safety offered by an honest connection to spirit. Whatever form that takes for you, an ability to confront the actual brevity and meaninglessness of all our endeavors and let that be simply so seems to help with the grace of simply letting go.

It may seem like both good news and bad, but alive, living, dying, or dead, none of the possibility for personal transformation goes away. Yet in a vaguely obtuse way, openings, or opportunities to transform do seem to rise closer to the surface and come more alive when people die.

Denying Death and Change

———

"There is a grace in denial.
It gives us a much needed break from the pain."
David Kessler

C hange always involves decay, death, and renewal. For
whatever reason, it feels natural to resist change, to
see it as a threat, to react to the heightening of our senses as an invitation for fear. Physiologically this causes a
parasympathetic response where the urge to flee or fight
naturally arises. Psychologically, conscious or not, another
reactive response is denial.

Whatever our response to a threat, real or existential,
the utility and validity of the parasympathetic part of that
response are unquestioned. To open to being with the very
many threats to humanity emerging in this century is quickly overwhelming, and it's natural to rush to judgment and
then react, acting first from this fight-or-flight response in

some attempt to preserve our chance to continue living. Or at least the hope for a chance that our grandchildren might be able to enjoy life in a verdant world.

Vanity such as this might become our downfall as a species. Lacking a capacity to go further before acting, far enough to be able to rest in the knowing that everything is okay, and if not really okay, impossibly and undeniably whole and complete right now as it is. Gaining access to this knowing, however, is still probably not enough to effectively support any real sustenance or long-term sustainability.

How can we be brilliant in our response to threats while not abandoning the wisdom and perspective that serves the bigger picture as well? Employing naivete, denial, indulgence in emptiness of hope, or sheer blind attempts to help ourselves or change others may temporarily allay the sense of immediate threat, but the collective result doesn't preclude destruction. It seems to me that developing a muscle of consciousness that allows for all the mistakes and messes to add up to something of value, becomes the possibility of a new normative way of existence that transforms the actual threat rather than blocking it.

I can't call this a new paradigm without scoffing at the arrogance of making such a claim for even if at least partially accurate in the assessment of qualities understood, this would be nothing more than viewing the path ahead as projected from the threshold of transformation, i.e., remaining attached to old, familiar, justifiably necessary ways of being in the past, while fantasizing about what it might be like "when we get there" in the future. Settling to only consider what such a future might be, I can collude and conspire to consider a "next" paradigm with anyone willing to attempt such honesty, but the longer I live, the less inspiring this endeavor becomes. After all, anything we hold as "future," no matter how hopeful, glorious, or apocalyptic, could never be more than a fantasy relative to what's so now. The concept of "future" is inadequate in leading to real change by its very construct as something that is not now. Sure, vision is absolutely valid and useful, but attachment to any such projection at the expense of fully feeling what there is to feel in the present is dangerously distracting.

Without digressing further, I bring this up here because of the way that Mary Lou's dying has helped me cultivate compassion for myself and others. She's dead now. And as I've related all manner of stories and emergence of new relatedness, I notice that opportunities for change and renewed understanding have all survived. Rather, all that stuff was already there and ultimately had little to do with her being alive or not.

Denial of a fact of reality like death is a normal and perhaps inevitable response. But to hang on to that as a foundation for what we build going forward is a choice. And one best not judged, only noticed and accepted. When we can accept our denial as part of our natural response and still confess the truth, the duality of all manner of false choices dissolves and we find that continuing a life of passion and meaning is still not only possible but happening now.

The Meaning of Life

———

Death without life is impossible.
Life without death is meaningless.

As humans, it seems we have a profoundly unique quality among the many species on our planet. This awareness of self or consciousness might feel like a personal matter, and it is, but not entirely in isolation. Rather, the existence of this humanness is made possible only through sharing and interactions based in the acknowledgment of our inherent interdependence.

Much of the strife in our world today is all the evidence we need of this. For me, a common theme among the many social issues surfacing and resurfacing today is how, when looking beyond the facts of injustice, anger, and hate, the real suffering seems to stem from insisting on being separate or deeming others different from us. Is the urge to uprise and outcry more a response to an unveiling of our inherent connectedness? A truth becoming undeniable clashing with our inner beliefs about who we are and how we relate to others? Maybe we're being called to become more honest with ourselves and others about the utter totality of our connectedness with all things. I really have to sit with it carefully as often, I can see both sides of an issue and feel trapped by false choice in the face of what feels like fighting over the unresolved trauma of having acted as though we were separate for so long.

Being even partially present to death, especially of someone we have loved and shared much of our life with, will sooner or later present challenges to our best efforts to maintain this illusion of separateness for which, as always, we have a choice in how we respond. In this respect, the beauty of death's seductive mystery is that, for better or worse, even if only for a moment, it brings people together. It envelops us with an opportunity to set aside judgments and differences with a measure more ease and grace than on a "life as usual" day and come face to face with those we otherwise have chosen to ignore. Death's affirmation and promise of life as precious and immutable provides an ultimate safety, if we allow it, to be with anyone.

In a recent discussion with a new friend and former minister about this book, he related how after officiating a great many weddings and funerals, he personally found much more meaningful resonance and joy in the funerals.

Not to diminish the celebration of embarking on a journey of love that a wedding is at all, this made complete sense.

Like the way our naked bodies are both beautiful and ugly, the perspective that sharing dying offers is like a knoll of truth where anyone can gather with a tacit agreement of a détente of sorts for all the meaninglessness of love and conflict and standing together to watch the story of a human life fade as the light from the setting sun gives way to the stillness of night.

The stories of our lives are crafted as made up meaning as we go, meaningless as they actually are. Their existence, however, is a source of renewal holding the possibility of our rebirth each time retold as a weaving of old and new. One of the chances we have in approaching dying with grace, whether the "diee" or "dier" is to concede the transference of authority in who is telling the story. While nothing really changes when one surrenders their voice in dying, its absence as the echo of meaning now reverberates through others offers a revelation of our collective and undivided humanity.

The Burden of Being Alive

—

"When it is darkest, we can see the stars."
Ralph Waldo Emerson

Having been through this with Mary Lou and Dad remains a source of ground for me in nurturing my own will to live. My own journey with the questions of "What do I have to live for?" and "Why am I here?" has never more clearly been encouraged by just knowing for starters that I *am* here now and any "why" and "what for" about that are things I can choose to create or not.

In watching how Mary Lou's fans and well-wishers danced with her decision, I was reminded that all of us have at least thought about the idea of suicide if not dared at points to consider the idea of doing so ourselves. This seems an ultimate consideration of embracing a will to live or not.

For me, while I'd developed enough facility with the space to ably support others who've told me they were planning or attempting to kill themselves, those thoughts have only reached a level of seriousness personally on a couple of occasions in my life, most recently in 2017 when I felt I couldn't go on without making a more conscious choice to be alive.

More a proactive consideration than a reaction to feelings of desperation, I was in my early years of recovery from alcohol and drug addiction and confronting how the manifestation of that disease had already been a version of killing myself. I had to accept how weak and pathetic I felt seeing that I had decided somewhere inside that I couldn't go on living yet didn't have the clarity to do more than maintain a living version of having already checked out. Also, given my upbringing in a social context that valued both environmental (the eco version) as well as spiritual health, I next had to confront the more prudent-feeling question of "Would the world be better off without me here?"

In the depths of this existential struggle to find if I had the strength to choose self-worth, I had to loosen my grip on the idea that humanity (i.e., me) was the "problem" with the state of the world. This letting go had to be done with extreme discernment if I was to also maintain my belief and understanding that yes, the Anthropocene (era of earth's natural evolution with the human species in the mix) was in fact so far a time of destructive and eroding effect actually threatening the capacity of our planet to support us.

All that is more for another story, but Mary Lou's journey helped me affirm that a) there's no guarantee that we will survive as a species, in fact in the bigger picture, we won't anyway and the only question is for how long, b) none of that concern for the "future" near or far really matters except for how it might inform our next actions now, and c) the only thing I can do is to play out my destined role to my own human satisfaction until I do die, whenever and however that should occur. When I watched Mary Lou ready, willing, and at peace with dying, yet living in a temporary hell of pain, my own pain in being alive became something I knew I could live with.

Regarding my identification with those of us on the crusade for "sustainability" and somehow instigating a "regenerative" existence in harmony with our environment, etc., having found a personal path that satisfactorily confronted these questions so deeply and honestly, has left me clear that if I am part of the problem, insofar as that I'm still here, I can also be part of a solution. Now, awareness of my carbon footprint or my ultimately greedy participation in a failed economic system isn't something to rush to fix, or erase, or judge others for as these are reactionary impulses that are as much the source of the problem as anything else. I don't know what I'm going to do next month or next year, but I am clear that if I cultivate this most honest capacity to be present, I'll know what action to take next as the time comes.

Sometimes, this makes being alive feel like a burden, and sometimes it feels gloriously aligned with some universal truth. Whatever our fate as a species is, I can now willfully and without fear always return to the place of "here I am now... so what next?" This gives me freedom to continue my human life of making mistakes, engineering triumphs, and hopefully bearing witness to the wonder of it all along the way.

Love

——

Love is a field of being, constant and immutable.
To love is a choice, simple and without
purpose or obligation.

Mary Lou and Dad founded their marriage, their relationship, on an idea that their connection transcended life and death. An easily sweet enough sentiment
in theory, but below the surface idea of invoking an open
door to the possibility of a continuation of their connection after life lay a not so traditional framework for living
and dying that in many ways made Mary Lou's choice to
die of her own volition possible.

This belief, memorialized in their wedding vows, allowed her to choose her own death without risking the
strength of their life together as a lasting resource for
Dad's continuing life. In balance, it left Dad with the joy
and burden of carrying their connection forward in ways

that go beyond settling for memory, legacy, and other such past-based agreements made when choosing loss.

Mary Lou's dilemma in the end was seeing that in honoring her inseverable commitment to their love, to die was undeniably her next best act to choose. I believe her hope was that Dad would find ways to continue his journey alone, or at least without her here with him physically, that also honored this shared understanding of their eternal connection. At least this is the context I held for her request of me to support Dad in this once in a lifetime transition for both of them.

Mary Lou was painfully aware of her presence as a burden with respect to Dad's capacity to continue growing and thriving for himself and rested the weight of her decision on the idea that her physical departure could be a gift of freedom for him. Dad understood the practicality of this while also doing his best to be gentle with himself in facing the tectonic disruption of familiarity in his daily doings.

I've watched Dad embark on this new chapter in life, fortunate to have a natural strength of individuality and almost Zen-like level of acceptance. Actively employing his skills and values for ongoing learning and discovery, and at the same time challenged by how to continue nurturing their shared love. Keeping their connection real and present while also grieving the loss of everything they had come to know by being together physically for forty-plus years has been no easy task.

For me at least, if the sentiment of their vow to share a connection "for as long as we both shall love" were to continue, the second part of the sentence would be "with joy until we don't." Not assuming that love shared is immutable but rather a choice brings the power of autonomy back. Shared love doesn't survive without exercising freedom of choice.

So, as I see it, the gift of freedom Mary Lou intended for Dad in no way usurped his capacity to continue loving her. Her natural confirmation shunned the arrogance of any such idea. She knew that in death as it was in their life together, she could only leave that to him which was another sign of their undying unity. To be able to have life be over for her and move on knowing that life wasn't over for Dad was also a gift to herself. A most elevated form of self-love.

As they found their way to saying "goodbye" in those final weeks, any tension with respect to the change that was coming for each of them was relieved when they shared the simple exchange of "I don't want to leave you, but I have to go." And "I don't want you to leave, but I know you have to go."

Communication with the Dead

——

"In the garden of memory, in the palace of dreams. . .
that is where you and I shall meet."
Alice Through the Looking Glass

To experience or pursue any form of ongoing dialogue with those who have passed is natural. For me, any such exchange is something to approach with careful attention for just as any challenges in communication when they were alive sometimes brings unexpected messages to decode and integrate, the continuance of a practice of speaking and listening is best tended to with enough courage to hear what I am able to and honor their right to express, doing my best to listen beyond any veils of obligation or indebtedness. Knowing that their lasting presence for me can continue to reveal opportunities to learn and grow bears no need to understand how or why right away at least.

In the depths of grieving, as powerful waves of emotion arrive with no schedule, washing over me with crests of joy and love and troughs of sorrow and despair, seeking the peace of acceptance is like waiting for grains of sand to wash up and settle in their new resting place on a beach. While feeling the lack of control in the matter can be disconcerting to say the least, I'm at least mildly comforted to remember that I was never in control to begin with.

It's only been a little over a year now in Dad's "new" life without Mary Lou's physical presence, and I continue to hold the space for him to find the sometimes rough edges of opportunity for continued growth to be both "normal" and easier to trust.

Not everyone is amenable to the pursuit of direct communication with the spirits of those who have passed. While one's motivation to pursue mediumship to this end is understandable, the idea is unfortunately mostly unacceptable on a societal level.

Alternatively, to shut the door more quickly on the recently passed, willfully deciding the connection severed permanently, and "move on," striving to replace the missing of formerly "normal" life is an equally valid choice. But for me, that is also sacrificial and something that Dad, in his cherished embodiment of a continued relationship with Mary Lou, would never do.

There are many who don't see death as the ending of a relationship, even to the point of seeking direct continued verbal communication with a belief they are still present and available for that. For these people, ongoing interaction is invited, hoped for, sought, and experienced. Seeing signs, feeling their presence, being visited in dreams, noticing butterflies, employing the mouthpiece of a medium, smelling their unique scent, hearing their voice. Dad has brought consistent and very focused intention to inviting and realizing new connections with Mary Lou since her death and has shared many experiences of her reciprocation and presence.

Our capacity to understand or accept some level of soul connection that transcends death, if needing conclusive evidence, finds explanation as proof, peaceful confirmation, coincidence, or simple grace. As personal and private as intimate details in a relationship ever are, there can be difficulties in sharing these experiences with others. Showing one's enthusiasm and joy in discovering such connections from "beyond the veil" easily clashes with differences in others' fundamental beliefs and ethos and whether thought through or not an awkward discomfort can arise.

Personally, I have no problem accepting the validity of these experiences but also have no need to make meaning that imposes existential challenges on others. I keep my opinions private mostly, and when others share such phenomena, I strive to cultivate a safe space for them to explore out loud. Truthfully, I enjoy listening to these stories of gratitude and love or pain and confusion. I understand the urge to share such revelatory experiences and have compassion for how doing so can disrupt sometimes long-held friendships and stability in family relationships. I've found there is a measure more ease in sharing less about an experience of disembodied connection and more about what it means to us.

For me, I can't accept that souls don't inhabit our world of conscious experience regardless of physicality or life or death status. I find comfort and an enticing tingle of mystery, or what I relate to as an unknowable unknown, in holding that my soul is more an "ours" thing, already existing beyond time and space, beyond before and after, beyond life and death. So why wouldn't I have access to an expressed identity of those who have passed? And conversely, why wouldn't *they*, on occasion, find *me* from wherever they are in the nowhere/everywhere of their disembodied habitude?

More interesting to me though is the question "What does one do with this ethereal knowing?" If the truth is ever present in some grand soup of souls that mingle, both defined and undefined as separable entities, so what? I could easily long for a resurrection of familiarity through a confirmed reconnection. Would this be motivated by refusal to accept the chance to release and move on alone or simply out of a natural and sweet desire to stay connected? I could react to any possible brush of energy from "the other side" with curiosity and joy, or with resistance and fear. If honest enough, it takes active intention and work to welcome any opportunity to continue nurturing an active relationship toward a hopeful unwinding of tensions and opening to more unity, acceptance, forgiveness, ownership, or love. I could even go further and endeavor to carry forth as a channel or conduit for anything perhaps still desired by the "other" deemed yet unresolved, or potentially valuable in its continued expression in "this plane."

No matter the nature or form of communication the exchange takes, for me it's important to consider: what do I have to say? Am I open to listening? Setting aside my need to identify and label whether what I "hear" back is an echo from the past, a creation of what I wish or hope they could or would say, or some new and possibly surprising message I haven't yet heard is helpful. In any case, the act of engaging in dialogue is as precious as it was when they were alive and there is nothing wrong with trying.

When I do make time to engage with my dead friends and relatives, I now ask questions of myself first. What do I need or want from you, from this present exchange? Comfort? Reassurance? Confirmation of our love continued? Healing acknowledgment or atonement for perceived or actual wrongs or harm imparted during our time of shared living? Or something else? No different from communication with the living, dialogue with those who have passed is a mystery that only reveals its value in the moment when I reach out with a clear presence of mind and sit to share and listen together.

However, I notice that at least for now, I have let go of most of my curiosity and drive to make meaning out of these experiences of oneness. I find comfort and relief enough in being settled with not knowing. I have grown less eager to spend time assessing, judging, labeling, and deciding what to understand as these activities seem only to drain my energy and take me away from just being here now.

Do all these "visitations" still happen? Of course! But that they do doesn't have to run me as much as simply exist to reveal something new and joyfully surprising (or dreadfully deflating, no difference) when they do. As with those I can still reach out to by text, phone, Zoom, or just dropping by their home; the choice to engage is mine alone and there is no "should" about whether I decide to or not.

It's enough for me to just return to stillness and gaze through the window, or "looking glass" until, like Alice, the frame dissolves and everything just is, complete and satisfactory in its paradoxical unity.

My New Dad

——

"I had seen birth and death but
had thought they were different."
T. S. Eliot

For me, the most challenging time in navigating a loss of this magnitude comes all too quickly after a memorial when the rest of the world so easily returns to life as usual, and we find ourselves alone and filled with what's no longer there. The ever-present reminders continue to smack us out of any illusion that we're coping fine, revealing the tenuous and tender nature of our fresh wound. Our habits of reaching out and seeking companionship, advice, or just to share might continue to initiate but seem to just trigger another empty echo from the void of counterpoint missing. Slowly, new gifts emerge with enough consistency to be reliable allies for gratitude shared and new life embraced.

After Mary Lou passed, I was eager to put in place supporting underpinnings of a new life for Dad. Knowing it was ultimately his work to do, I also knew I could provide encouragement and guidance while I was still at Elysian Hills with him. This was all aided by the sense of underlying excitement that we shared for the room we had now created for a deeper relationship as father and son.

As the first week unfolded, I did my best to support Dad in transforming the energy of his home and life enough to anchor something new and different as a context for his daily activities. We got out Dad's beloved chainsaw and, in defiance of Mary Lou's demand that he stop using it, we dispatched a dying tree that was getting ready to come down on its own soon and positioned in threat of landing on the power lines and/or house on its way. We shared in the darkish humor that we were given license in this case because her demand was moot as it was a living one and now, nearly literally "over her dead body," it was somehow okay.

We moved his office from the separate building it had been in for more than thirty years into the house in the back of the living room where Mary Lou had her desk and computer. We removed a tired couch and rearranged the family living room so Mary Lou's empty chair, where she had spent the majority of her time, wasn't tripped over both literally and emotionally every time when entering the room.

We started enjoying going out to eat, trying new restaurants Dad and Mary Lou hadn't gone to together. I even changed the swing of the refrigerator door, something I had been suggesting, out of practicality for years, but now felt compelled to just do. We caught up on a few winterizing tasks around the property that had by now been deferred well past their normal schedule.

We talked about the term *widower* and how that new label felt like a fit or not. Knowing he didn't "need" my help but doing it anyway, I made a plea to some of his closest friends to promise to reach out, especially if they hadn't heard from Dad in a while. Suggesting a call, or just to drop by the house or invite him to lunch or coffee in town saying, "I know he'd appreciate spending time with you but might not be able to ask for it himself."

Mary Lou had asked me to "help Dad through the transition" and anticipating Dad might not have much motivation for furniture moving and such, I knew that doing these things right away would support positive new patterns in the long run.

No one could ever replace Mary Lou's presence in Dad's daily life, and it would be absurd and disrespectful to think that possible. But he could find, in the space now left open, new people, new relationships, new passions and projects that he felt (hopefully) worth living for.

I could see that any hope I was hanging onto for him was probably more a projection of my own desperation in finding meaning in my life. I knew I could only offer my love and if he wanted to share in that space with me, we might both be able to heal forward.

We have done just that together in the months and now years since Mary Lou's passing.

Epilogue

—

This book is my own exploration of what it might be like to die consciously and the realization that this inquiry invokes only a practice of conscious living.

The dozen or more experiences of being witness to dear beings in my life dying in 2021 and 2022 still offer an abundance of opportunity for me to stop and pay attention to my own life. Just living with and through each loss privately would have been impactful enough, changing and shaping me in meaningful ways as I look forward to my last few decades alive if that comes to pass. But something about the way Mary Lou approached and embraced her own life and death compelled me to also write my way through to deeper understanding and share it with you. I'm glad I did.

I feel I've but scratched the surface, but the shining insight I hope is clear to you through reading this is how much Mary Lou came alive when she decided to die. For years before that decision, at least from my point of view, I could see her life force dwindling. Perhaps on the order of slow change that goes unnoticed by those closest to her on a daily basis, her demeanor increasingly showed signs of apathy that betrayed and frayed her stalwart commitment to a positive attitude. I would have had no difficulty at all watching her will to live just appear to drain out as I used to think was normal for the elderly who were "lucky" enough to live so long. I probably would have felt sorry for her and colluded with others in how "at least she lived a full life, etc.," speaking in the past tense before she had even died!

All those ideas have now surfaced and have been shattered by what I saw through her path of choice. The moment she decided to die and put that plan into action, she didn't fade away at all. She fully came back to life! Flourishing in every way, energized and brimming, not just being alive while waiting to die anymore but full of *life*!

Seeing this, I can't go back to any conscious or subconscious fear of losing my life force before I die. This experience has changed me in ways I will surely continue to discover for the rest of my life. I am filled with gratitude and wonder for new choices and possible actions I now might take, or not, along the way.

I find myself asking: What changes when one finds one is ready to stop living and start dying? Will I know when I'm ready to really start dying? Will I choose to share that experience with others? With whom? How? I'm happy to honestly say I don't know and curiously don't care to for now. I am settled to have at least established that I'm not afraid of asking. Maybe that's enough.

Spending time pondering and processing some of the truths around living and dying in this way has thankfully brought me beyond any urge to draw conclusions and create some neat and tidy box of understanding to put on the shelf. I suppose I've carried a fear that my reverence for these experiences would fade, and I would revert to barreling ahead with my own life, paying less attention to the moment-by-moment mystery of it all daily.

I could choose to be grateful to have reached some level of comfort with the topic through having spent something like six months now committing this exploration to the writing of this book. But having done so, I'm only present to how the questions that have arisen to dance with are most life-giving when I leave them unanswered.

This way, the mysteries of the meaning of life continue to unfold for me whenever I find the desire, strength, and time to indulge my curiosity and explore more. For this I'm grateful. To have decided for myself that "this" or "that" is so about life would have shuttered the possibility of these openings tighter and left me with just a new version of the buried discomfort I began with. At least I now have something in having told this story to return to whenever I choose to sit at these windows again and gaze for new perspectives and what they might reveal next.

Also, I can't overlook that one of the main reference points along the journey shared here is grief. Like a loyal companion in any conversation about death, the power of grief, whether through how it seems to have its way with us like it or not, or through grieving with intention, is perhaps more the palette of colors one draws from to paint any landscape of understanding of life. Navigating my own grieving for all the recent losses I've experienced while writing a book about conscious dying has left me with one question I'm eager to explore next. What changes when one has passed?

This exploration probably begins with how the mystery, pain, and joy of losing loved ones has changed me and continues to do so. I've come to see grief as intimately connected with love and bliss but that knowing has never changed the depth of bewildering confusion and embodied despair that comes with the territory.

Sure, there are many tips and tools and useful mental frameworks to at least keep things "on the rails" as we tumble in grief hoping for a return to solid ground. All that is very useful, but the hurt remains real while it is there. To allow the vast empty sadness to be enough for now with its own raw beauty filling the hole of loss is, unfortunately it seems, a lost art in our culture.

I have many experiences to share regarding what it is to anticipate grief, be in grieving, and look back on having grieved. There is so much to grieve for in our world today, and I can't imagine how much more loss is still to come for all of us. I think we all would do well to learn to grieve with a measure more intention and allowing.

That is another story, a different expedition entirely.

So, for now, thank you, Mary Lou and Dad.

And thank you Mom, Murphee, Mark, Jeff, Ruth, John, Tracy, Yoenny, Auntie Bea, Little Dennis, Brian, Mel, and Taylor. And Bill, Uncle Bill, Chuck, Sean, Alberta, Sukee, Rosee, Gerry, Caspian, Tyler, Jenny, Sweet Pea, La, Festus, Naomi, and others whose names I don't remember.

May you rest in peace and all your deaths continue to fill the world with newfound life.

Selfie of Paul and his dad two weeks after Mary Lou had passed and minutes before Paul left the farm for home in Wyoming, leaving him alone at the house for the first time.

Afterword

———

With appreciation and encouragement, I thank you for going on this journey with me.

As solely individual as each life is, there are a vast range of experiences with losing a loved one, each one deeply personal and unique by circumstance and design, like snowflakes, similar yet entirely unique. The mysteries any of us confront each time a death occurs, and each time we revisit the experience are rife with seeds of value that germinate and flourish when we explore them with others. Please find the time and create the language to share about your feelings regarding death with people you love and care about. I'm certain your life and theirs will be better for it.

I could only have been able to relate this story now for the relative baseline of acceptance I perceive our society holds for the natural death of a ninety-five-year-old woman at peace with her own completeness in life. It's common when a long life comes to a reasonably natural close to share a sense of relief and celebration alongside the wrenching emptiness and existential pallor that arrives with the loss. The balance of these common emotional responses, combined with a level of societal grace for the elderly, makes it easier to write about in cases like this.

Surprise deaths are so different. Losing a child, dog, best friend, mentor, or anyone close all of a sudden has taught me something of the trauma that can accompany untimely and unanticipated loss. It is challenging to access the beauty, but it's there along with the heightened sense of utter obliteration of self that those types of grief journeys bring.

I find peace in holding compassion and reverence for whatever you might be experiencing as you review past, current, or future deaths in your life. It brings me a measure of shared pain, like scratching a scar or massaging a past wound, when I consider what you might be going through that sometimes feels so real and raw it's difficult to confront. I also know that you might be finding new access to deeper layers of healing, and that is something to celebrate.

I do, again, invite you to share with me, if you're so moved, about your experiences with death and dying. I truly love this conversation and would be profoundly grateful to learn of anything you may have discovered in reading this. In any case, I hope that my offering of companionship can be received for the simple yet inadequate feeling of silent anticipation it holds.

Exploring the landscape of what follows a death, and the vision quest grieving can be is entirely another story, but for now, may this account change you in ways that help you be more present with anyone in your life (including *you*) as we all live and die.

With sincere love and gratitude,

paulschmidtauthor@gmail.com

About the Author

—

After growing up in Vermont, Paul Schmidt moved to the Rocky Mountain West in 1989. He now lives at the confluence of three rivers in the mountains of rural Wyoming. Paul enjoys ultra-marathon trail running, working in his wood shop, and traveling with his wife and two Australian shepherds Lilee and Kaytee.

A lifelong student of human/eco dynamics, he participated in the Science in Society Project at Wesleyan University and studied human ecology and holistic health at the University of Vermont, graduating with a BA in Environmental Awareness. He published the *Whole Health Directory, a guide to wellness practitioners in northern Vermont, Geneva and the Environment: A Guide to International Environmental Activity and Organizations*, and a free quarterly publication called *Conscious Times*.

He is a visionary leader and determined realist. His talent and passion for connecting people and positive ideas worldwide has engaged a diverse range of clients, employers, and partners, including non-profit organizations, educational institutions, product companies, foundations, hospitality organizations, membership associations, and individuals. Paul likes to see his best accomplishments manifest through the work of others, and his influence has spurred evolutionary change in global environmental management, and the wellness, hospitality, regenerative business, and conscious leadership industries.